BYGONE RYE AND WINCHELSEA

Bygone
RYE
and
WINCHELSEA

Aylwin Guilmant

Phillimore

1984

Published by
PHILLIMORE & CO. LTD.
Shopwyke Hall, Chichester, Sussex

ISBN 0 85033 534 5

Printed and bound in Great Britain by
BILLING & SONS LTD
Worcester, England

LIST OF ILLUSTRATIONS

This book is dedicated
to
the people of Winchelsea and Rye,
both past and present

PREFACE

This book does not set out to be a history of these two 'antient' (*sic*) towns; rather it is a story of their people who throughout the ages have created for us history in our midst. Many of the buildings remain little altered and by a short stretch of the imagination it is possible to be transported back in time to a less turbulent age than the present. In portraying a way of life that perhaps sadly is no longer with us, I salute those worthy inhabitants who created towns such as these for those coming after to enjoy.

ACKNOWLEDGEMENTS

I would like to thank Mr. G. S. Bagley, Curator of Rye Museum, for his help, the Record Office at Lewes, East Sussex County Library at Brighton, *The Bexhill Observer, Hastings & St Leonards Observer* and Mrs. Mary Owen of *The Rye Gazette.* I am indebted to Mrs. Pamela Haines, the Bexhill Area Librarian, who placed much useful information at my disposal. Especial thanks must go to the following who gave most generously of their time and help in so many ways: Miss Sheila Axell, Mrs. Josephine Kirkham and Mr. Frank Palmer of Rye, together with Mr. Alan Dickinson of Playden. The photographic work for the book was carried out by Mr. Ewan J. Walder and I am most grateful for his willing and cheerful help often given at very short notice; without his expertise none of this would have been possible. I would like to thank the following for permission to use certain of their photographs and other relevant material: Mr. D. H. Turner, Mayor of Winchelsea 1982-3 and 1983-4, Mr. C. C. Croggan, Town Clerk and Miss Josie Andrew, all connected with Winchelsea Museum; also Miss M. Cullwick of this town and Mr. Lofthouse, headmaster of Winchelsea School. I am also deeply indebted for the kind and willing co-operation of many people, too numerous to mention individually, who have so generously lent pictures from their family albums, without which this book would not have been possible.

The following institutions kindly provided illustrations: The Public Record Office (by permission of the Controller H.M.S.O., Crown Copyright Reserved) nos. 1, 96, 112, 114; Trustees of the British Museum no. 4; the Central Library, Brighton nos. 6, 7, 8, 12, 15, 16, 20, 24, 25, 31, 33, and 107; the Martello Bookshop nos. 27 and 28 (copyright reserved); Rye Museum Association nos. 30, 48, 59, 62, 65, 80, 87, 91, 93, 94, 95, and 113; Alan Jones no. 99; the *Hastings Observer* no. 69; the Library of Harvard University no. 97; Winchelsea Museum nos. 101-150 (except no. 113); and The British Engineerium Steam Museum, Hove no. 76.

BIBLIOGRAPHY

General

Armstrong, J. R., *The History of Sussex* (1974)
Bagley, G. S., *A Connoisseur's Guide to Rye* (1979)
Bagley, G. S., *Edwardian Rye* (1974)
Bagley, G. S., *William Holloway* (1963)
Bagley, G. S., *The Book of Rye* (1982)
Brandon, Peter, *The Sussex Landscape* (1974)
Clark, K. M., *100 Years of Town Guides* (1965)
Clark, K. M., *Smuggling in Rye and District* (1977)
Collard, J. A., *A Maritime History of Rye* (1978)
Cooper, W. D., *The History of Winchelsea* (1850)
Hinings, Edward, *History, People & Places in The Cinque Ports* (1975)
Holloway, W., *The History and Antiquities of the Ancient Town and Port of Rye* (1847)
Holloway, W., *Antiquarian Rambles through Rye* (1863 and 1866)
Horsfield, T., *The History, Antiquities and Topography of the County of Sussex* (1835)
Hyde, H. Montgomery, *The Story of Lamb House* (1975)
Lovegrove, H., *The Official Guide to the Antient* [sic] *Town of Winchelsea* (1979)
MacLean, Homan W., *A Short Account of the History and Antiquities of Winchelsea* (1936)
Murray, W. J. C., *Romney Marsh* (1972)
Nairn, I. and Pevsner, N., *Sussex — Buildings of England* (1965)
Sussex Archaeological Collections (Lewes), vol. 13
The Sussex Genealogist, vol. 4, No. 3
Victoria County History, vol. 2 and vol. 9.
Vidler, L. A., *A New History of Rye* (1934; and reprinted 1971)
Vine, P. A. L., *The Royal Military Canal* (1972).

Guide Books

Ward Lock & Co. (1923)
Black's *Guide to Kent* (1882)
Adams' *Guide to Rye and District*, c. 1938
Deacon's *Illustrated Guide to Rye*, c. 1900
The Story of Winchelsea Church, 18th ed.
Rye Parish Church of St Mary the Virgin (1974)
Rye Colour Guide (1982)

Newspapers

East Sussex Express (various copies)
Hastings Observer (various copies)
Sussex Weekly Advertiser or Lewes Journal (9 September 1782)
The Rye Gazette
Rye's Own Magazine

Article

'Rye Church Clock', E. J. Tyler (reprinted from *Antiquarian Horology*, Winter 1976)

Rye

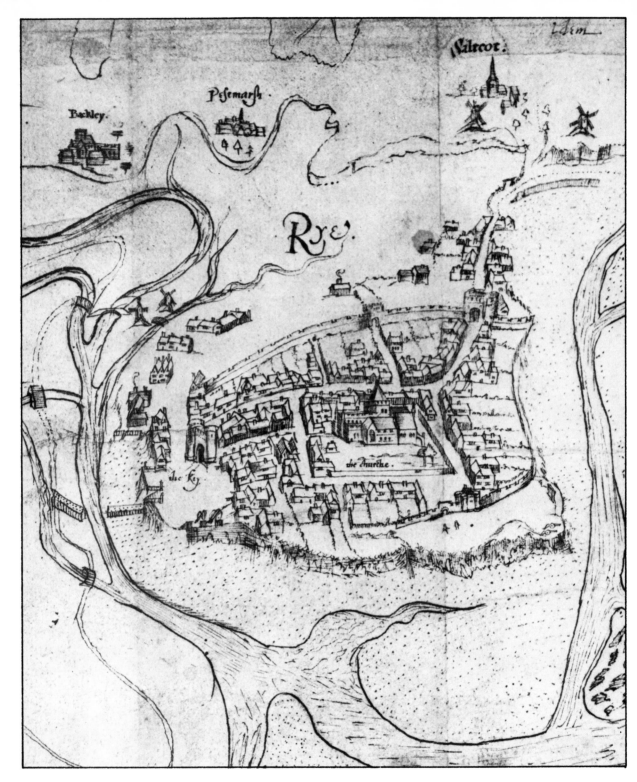

1. Detail from the 16th-century map by Philip Symonsen from the south. The various gates into the town can be clearly seen, likewise the church of St Mary the Virgin and the town walls which at one time surrounded Rye.

RYE – INTRODUCTION

THE ANCIENT AND ROMANTIC town of Rye, like Winchelsea, formed part of the lands of the Norman abbey of Fecamp even before the Norman Conquest, and was still held by the abbey when the Domesday Book was compiled in 1086. In 1247 Henry III negotiated for the return of these lands and Rye became a royal manor. It then became a royal borough, with a mayor and a bailiff, each of whom was entitled to their own mace as a symbol of authority.

The town stands on a rocky eminence not far from the Kentish boundary, and it was at one time almost entirely surrounded by water. Today these waters have receded, and broad stretches of marshland have replaced the rolling tide. Many of Rye's characteristics seem more Flemish than English, and it is interesting to notice that an early form of its name – *Rieberg*, 1085 – echoes this resemblance. Other names for the town appear to stem from words meaning 'island', although an alternative theory suggests that 'Rye' derives from the French word *rue* meaning 'a road'.

The so-called 'golden age' of Rye occurred in the 13th and 14th centuries, when trade thrived. Wood from the Weald of Sussex and Kent was shipped out from the town to various continental ports; fish was sent to London; and continental goods, such as salt, cider, oil and Gascony wine were imported. Edward I granted the town an annual fair in 1290, to be held on the Feast of the Nativity of the Virgin, and all traders at the fair enjoyed special privileges for the seven years following their attendance at it. Besides the fair, the town had a thriving market, wind and watermills, and a pottery.

The town benefited greatly from the great storm of 1287 which, as we shall see, completely submerged the port of Old Winchelsea. The course of the river Rother, which previously had its outlet to the sea at New Romney, was changed, and it now discharged its waters into Rye Bay, close to the town itself. While Winchelsea was struggling to re-establish itself on a new site, Rye became guardian of the mouth of their joint harbour (see Vidler, *A New History of Rye*, 1934).

In 1336 Rye was granted full membership of the Cinque Ports confederation. The special status of the ports originated in their undertaking to perform 'ship service', which meant that the seven ports supplied a certain number of manned and equipped ships for the King's service. This undertaking was of course particularly valuable in time of war. Every man who contributed to fitting out ships for the Cinque Port fleet was entitled to certain privileges: these men were originally known as 'portsmen', but later took the title 'baron'. They had their own Courts of Justice, which were the only places where they could be sued. They paid no taxes to the King; they were free to buy and sell at all the various markets in the kingdom; and their trading vessels were exempt from harbour dues in all ports.

After Rye and Winchelsea joined the confederation, its official title became 'the Cinque Ports and the Two Ancient Towns'. According to G. S. Bagley, in his book *A Connoisseur's Guide to Rye* (1979), this appellation was used prior to chief port status, but the reason for it is not known.

Rye, like the other Cinque Ports, was governed internally by a set of Ordinances known as the Custumal. William Holloway, the historian of Rye, states that 'the Ports, in their corporate character, were all equally bound by the Charters; but each Port, in its individual character, had the power of framing by-laws for its own internal government. This code of laws was called the Custumal, and each town had its own, which was designated as the Custumal of that particular town'. (From *The History and Antiquities of the Ancient Town and Port of Rye*, which was written in 1847, p. 137). At one time a copy of the Rye Custumal was preserved in the town hall; although it was written in 1564, it is clear that it was copied from an earlier document of about 1415. The Custumal did not only deal with matters relating to the duties of officials and those in authority, but it also protected the 'freemen' or 'barons' when they were travelling in other parts of the country. Although the title of 'Cinque Ports baron' remains today, its holders are drastically reduced in number, being limited to the mayors or law officers of the towns concerned, appointed at a royal coronation.

Rye was not untouched by the great religious movements of the 13th and 14th centuries. An order of friars known as the Brothers of the Repentance of Jesus Christ (or more popularly as the 'Brothers of the Sack') were granted permission as early as 1263 to dwell in Rye. It is interesting to notice that Jews were also given this right, but it is thought that in their case they gained the privilege by virtue of a payment of money!

Medieval Rye did not escape misfortunes, brought upon it by natural disaster and through the actions of man. The French paid several uninvited visits and wrought great havoc on at least four occasions. Following one such attack in 1377, when the town was sacked and burnt, the townsfolk entreated King Richard II 'to have consideration of the poor town of Rye, inasmuch as it has several times taken . . . and is unable further to repair the walls, wherefore the town is, on the seaside, open to enemies'. The French burnt down the magnificent church, and looted and pillaged. Local indignation rose so high in consequence that some of the leading inhabitants were hung, drawn and quartered because it was felt that they had neglected the town's defences. In 1377 the French had left the church a roofless ruin and stolen the bells: the following year the men of Rye had their revenge when they in turn sacked towns in Normandy — and recovered their church bells.

However, the town also suffered damage and destruction at the hands of nature. The eastern flats were inundated by the sea, and part of the town was swept away, including the chapel and manse of St Austin. The friars who lived there were forced to begin again on a new site, called 'La Haltone'.

Rye was visited twice by the Black Death in the 14th century, once in the great nationwide outbreak of 1348-9 and then again between 1360 and 1369. Further outbreaks of plague periodically decimated Rye even into the 17th century, when for a period of 11 years the burials in the parish register exceeded the baptisms by 158, a statistic which clearly reveals the frightful ravages made by the dreaded disease — although some of these deaths may have been due to other epidemics, such as smallpox and the sweating sickness (see *Sussex Arch. Coll.*, vol. 13, pp. 180-208).

In the 15th century, Rye's fortunes began to decline. This was partly because the Cinque Ports as a whole were not so important as they had been in the past. With the development of large shipyards elsewhere their small fleet was bound to seem somewhat parochial. John Collard says in *A Maritime History of Rye* (1978), that the 'influence of Rye in the sphere of international commerce and warfare steadily declined'. It is thought that Rye reached her lowest sphere of depression at about the time when Tenterden was incorporated into the town. The latter was a rich and important town with a thriving landing at Smallhythe, sited less than ten miles from Rye. Tenterden was appointed as a 'limb' of Rye in 1449 when the latter was unable to meet her quota of ships as a Cinque Port, following further French raids on the town. Between 1485-8 Rye had lost all her remaining trading vessels: these had previously constituted the town's chief source of wealth through its profitable trade with continental ports. Samuel Jeake (Rye's 17th-century historian) tells us that 'Rye never recovered its ancient shipping since the loss of the Bordeaux fleet [i.e., a fleet of ships bound for Bordeaux] as reported in the time of King Henry VII'. Jeake puts no date on the affair, nor does he tell us whether the fleet was captured by the enemy or wrecked in a storm, although the latter does seem the most plausible explanation (see Holloway's *History*).

By the middle of the 16th century, most trade had fallen into the hands of foreigners: it is said that 37 'hoys' sailed out of Rye on one tide, laden with timber from the Weald, and never an English mariner amongst them. These foreign sailors were mostly Flemings. Rye outfitted one ship for Queen Elizabeth's fleet when it sailed to meet the Spanish Armada, but her men took no part in the battle (see Vidler).

Later in the 16th century the town's economic situation worsened still further, owing to the deteriorating condition of its rivers and harbour. Much of this may have been due to the 'inning' of certain of the marshes, a process which had been going on since the 11th century. 'Inning' or draining reduced the tidal flow, and thus the outfall ultimately became blocked. William Camden, in his *Brittania*, written towards the end of Queen Elizabeth's reign, noted that Rye 'beginneth to complain that the sea abandoneth it'.

However, Rye was still considered well worth defending, and in 1539 King Henry VIII built Camber Castle to command the entrance to the port. It cost £23,000 to build; the revenue for it was derived from the wealth of the suppressed monasteries and other religious houses in the area, and the actual stone used also came from these buildings. In 1541 the castle was armed with artillery, and a captain was appointed, who was under the command of the Constable of Dover Castle. Ypres Tower, originally built for defensive purposes, had passed into private hands during the 15th century, but in 1518 the Corporation of Rye re-purchased it for £26. It was then described as 'Baddings Towre alia Ipres Tower'. Later in its history it became the town gaol.

In 1562-3 the first bands of Protestant refugees from Catholic persecution began to arrive from the Continent. Unfortunately, their arrival coincided with another outbreak of plague, and 562 burials took place in the town during 1563. However, the town's population was soon augmented by further refugees, fleeing after the St Bartholomew's Day Massacre in 1572. By the end of the century there were 1,534 persons of French extraction living in Rye. Rye, like Winchelsea, owed its weaving industry to these refugees (see *Sussex Arch. Coll.*, vol. 13).

Queen Elizabeth I visited Rye in 1573. She stayed for three days, and on her departure gave it the name of 'Rye Royal'. In return, the town presented her with 100 golden angels. Six years later Rye was the birthplace of the dramatist John Fletcher, perhaps best known for his successful collaboration with William Beaumont. Fletcher's father was Vicar of Rye, but he himself was only two years old when the family left the town.

Samuel Jeake, Rye's first historian, was born in the town in 1623. His account of contemporary and past events in the town has proved an invaluable source for all later writers on the town. His father suffered much in life: according to a recent writer on Rye (G. S. Bagley), 'the one calm period he enjoyed was during the Interregnum, with perhaps 1651 being the most satisfactory year of his life, when he became a freeman of Rye and its Common Clerk'. Left a widower with two small sons, he early instilled into his son of the same name an abiding interest in the town of his birth. The father produced *Charters of the Cinque Ports*, which contained the first descriptive account of Rye, while the son compiled his *Nativity*, a form of diary in which he recorded the events of his life. This younger Jeake became a merchant specialising in the import and export of goods to the Continent. Both were religious dissenters, and suffered for their beliefs; Samuel Jeake the elder had to leave Rye for a number of years.

A record of 17th-century Rye of another sort was provided by the famous Dutch painter, Sir Anthony Van Dyck, who stayed briefly in the town early in the century. He made a number of drawings there, which can be compared with those in the margins of the 1593 map of Philip Symonsen. Later in the century, another Dutchman, Jacob Esselens, drew Rye from the shoreline.

It is probable that the town had a grammar school in medieval times, but no evidence seems to have survived which could prove this. In 1638 a citizen of Rye, Thomas Peacocke, left money in his will for the founding of a free school for the boys of the town. Peacocke's School was established the following year, and was later immortalised as 'Pocock's Grammar School' in *Denis Duval*, a novel by W. M. Thackeray.

Another local landmark received long overdue repairs during the last years of the century. The church, a famous landmark for mariners, had almost become a complete ruin, but an appeal to the King brought £400 for repairs, which were carried out by 1703.

Throughout the Civil War, Rye was strongly Parliamentarian and Puritan in its sympathies. It was little affected by the actual fighting, although men from Rye joined the Parliamentarian army and took part in battles in other parts of the country.

In 1660 a census of the town was carried out, to assess its inhabitants for a tax. It lists 660 persons, with their occupations and the district in which they lived; besides these, who would have been the heads of households, there were of course women, children and old people who could no longer earn their own living. The largest single occupational group was that of sea trades.

A connection with the New World of America was established in 1660, when descendants of an inhabitant of Rye purchased land from the Indians and founded two villages in New York State, one called Rye and the other Hastings.

During the 18th century the notorious Hawkhurst smuggling gang was operating in Sussex. Rye was visited regularly by members of the gang. They could be seen 'carousing and smoking their pipes, with their loaded pistols lying on the tables before them, no magistrate daring to interfere with them' at hostelries like the *Mermaid* Inn, according to the historian William Holloway. Contemporary newspapers record cargo from smuggling cutters being conveyed to Rye Customs House, and sales notices exist which record goods being sold to the general public from here. The preacher John Wesley, who visited Rye more than once, recorded in his *Diary* on 22 November 1773 that Rye folk 'will not part with the accursed thing — smuggling'.

Some time after 1750, portions of the town walls were demolished, as was Strand Gate. Stones from these demolitions were incorporated into the new churchyard walls.

By the 18th century, Rye was a 'pocket borough', returning two Members of Parliament, the choice of whom was firmly controlled by the Duke of Newcastle. In 1717 we find the first mention of the Lamb family in the town records. This particular member of the family, and his descendants served as mayor on over 70 occasions. It was said that the Lamb family and their various relations virtually 'controlled' the town; the Grebell family could also boast an almost equally frequent appearance in office.

James Lamb was the mayor in 1725 and found himself unexpectedly host to a monarch. George I, on his way from Hanover to London, was forced by the bad weather to take refuge in Rye, his vessel having got into difficulties in Rye Bay. He stayed at Lamb House.

In 1741 Rye Town Hall was built to a design by Andrew Jelfe. An imposing building, it has an interesting feature in the Court Room, where the names of all the mayors of the town since 1286 are inscribed. In 1825 a 'sit-in' was staged in the Town Hall when a quarrel over an election led to there being two mayors — one the official one, the Reverend William Dobson (who was related to the Lamb family by marriage), and a rival claimant, John Meryon, who locked Dobson out of the Town Hall. He and his supporters remained in the Town Hall for six weeks before they were forced to vacate it and allow the reverend gentleman and his corporation to take office.

During the 18th century the Harbour Commissioners, with the help of a grant from Parliament, appointed John Smeaton (the engineer who had been responsible for Eddystone Lighthouse and Ramsgate Harbour) to develop a proposed new harbour for Rye. Due to a number of major problems, the work was finally abandoned in 1788; this move apparently met with the wholehearted support of the merchants, tradesmen, owners of vessels, fishermen and mariners of Rye, who all signed a grateful letter of thanks for the reopening of the old harbour of Rye!

The production of pottery had first begun in Rye in the 13th century, but there was a 400-year gap between these medieval activities and the re-establishment of a ceramics industry in the 18th century which has never been satisfactorily explained. The Rye pottery developed at the Cadborough brickworks as a sideline: they produced domestic ware as well as other objects such as tiles, chimney pots, sewer-pipes, and garden and farm utensils. One of the best of the early potters was William Mitchell, whose 'Hop Ware' goods are today highly prized by collectors (see Bagley, *Book of Rye*, pp. 108-9).

In 1778 the first stage coach (called the *Diligence*) ran from Rye to London, taking 15 or 16 hours for the journey. The inns of the town flourished with these improved communications, three of the busiest being the *George*, the *Red Lion* and the *Cinque Ports Arms*. Coach traffic went to the first, the post to the second, and the carrier business to the third (Bagley, p. 76). The inns served as centres for entertainment as well as hospitality. The fine assembly room at the *George* was opened in 1818, and at least one other Rye inn — the *Cinque Ports Arms* — could also boast an assembly room, complete with stage. Between 1800 and 1830 Rye also had a flourishing theatre, situated near to the present site of the Baptist chapel. The entertainments offered were varied, but all the theatre productions commenced with a 'dissertation' or comic monologue, and ended with a comic song. One such production was *Richard III*, which took place in January 1803. Not content with the play itself, the theatre also offered its public a further musical entertainment. All the proceeds of the evening were 'for the Benefit of the Poor'. The theatre bills, of which the museum holds a remarkable collection, are a triumph of the typographer's art and were printed in Rye itself.

By 1846, however, the stage coach had almost been put out of business by the advent of the railway. William Holloway, writing of communications between Rye and London in that year, commented that 'the present coach runs only to the railway station at Staplehurst, whither it goes in the morning and returns every night'. The previous year discussions had begun on the idea of bringing Rye its own station, on a line from Ashford through Rye to Hastings. In 1850 the Lord Mayor of London came in state to open the Swing Bridge which had been built to carry the railway over the River Rother, an event recorded in the *Illustrated London News*. A market and cattle yards quickly grew up around the station, and Rye became one of the largest and most prosperous markets in the south east.

In 1832 with the passing of the Parliamentary Reform Act, Rye lost one of its members of parliament, and shared the other with adjoining villages and the town of Winchelsea. She still, however, retained the preponderance of votes. The best known M.P. for Rye of the period was Arthur Wellesley, later to become the Duke of Wellington. In 1835 the Act to Provide for the Regulation of Municipal Corporations brought to an end the system under which the town had been governed internally since 1289.

The political life of Rye during the early and middle years of the 19th century was dominated by Jeremiah Smith, the Liberal agent and at one time mayor of the town. In 1852 an inquiry before the House of Commons was held into the alleged bribery of electors at Rye. Smith spent a year in Newgate following a conviction for perjury, but was subsequently reprieved. 'It must be conceded', writes G. S. Bagley, 'that Mr. Smith strode the Borough's stage for many years and established a typical electioneering machine — and no doubt, saw that the Municipal Corporations Act was put into operation in Rye in a manner that harmonised with the sentiments of the borough'. (*The Book of Rye*, 1982). Throughout the 18th and 19th centuries, elections were enlivened by the production of squibs, lampoons and other scurrilous election material full of personal innuendo and abuse, and the Rye printers were as active in this way as any.

With the building of the railway, the town continued to improve. Gas was laid, the water supply improved, and the Salts (which had previously been embanked) became a recreation ground. The two Free Schools in Rye united and by 1866 a National School had been built in Mermaid Street. In 1859 the Cinque Ports Volunteer Rifle Corps came into being, although as early as 1779 another body, called the Cinque Ports Volunteers Company, had been raised and subsequently disbanded. Later in its history the Rifle Corps was renamed the Cinque Ports Rifle Volunteers, members of which served with distinction in the Boer War.

During the 19th century many men and women began to develop what later became known as a 'social conscience'. One outcome of this new concern was the building of new almshouses in Military Road, and the opening of a soup kitchen for the poor, operating from a structure built against the Ypres Tower. Campaigns for social improvements were often stimulated by the press, and three local newspapers were established—the *Rye Chronicle, Rye Free Press,* and the *Rye Telegram*.

Rye's economic life was now once more in a healthy state. The middle years of the 19th century were the golden age of shipbuilding in the town; three yards were operating, specialising in the construction of sailing trawlers of the ketch type. The industry was centred around the small area of the Strand and the Rock Channel. During one three-year period (1852-5), 26 vessels were launched. These occasions made news in the national press of the time, and one of the vessels, the *Marian Zagury*, was featured in the *Illustrated London News*. Another Rye vessel, the schooner *Madeira Pet*, had the distinction of being the first European vessel to dock in the port of Chicago in 1850, and this event received full coverage from American newspapers. However, towards the end of the century shipbuilding declined, and the coasting vessels using the port decreased in number. Previously cargoes were despatched from Rye to European ports, whilst imports of wood and coal were received for distribution.

In 1888 Rye Regatta was revived, and this flourished for a number of years, providing inhabitants and visitors alike with a popular spectacle. As early as 1839, the town had had a steam ferry service to Boulogne, but this did not prove to be a viable enterprise and was withdrawn after a few years. Tourists could, however, enjoy trips on the river and up the neighbouring waterways. The vessels used for this purpose were also used for the transportation of goods locally, and had uniquely large rudders and tillers, suitable for negotiating the narrow reaches of the river.

Two local companies founded in the last century have sadly both gone today. These were the Rother Iron Works and the Rye Chemical Manufacturing Company, which both employed a large workforce. Rye Brewery has also closed down in the 20th century. Rye was formerly an important port for the distribution of hops, and the brewery produced beer from locally-grown hops.

During the last decade of the 19th century a golf course was constructed at Camber, and the Rye and Camber Tramway was constructed, connecting the club with the Monkbretton Bridge. Whilst the golf course is still considered to be one of Britain's finest coastal courses, the tramway ceased to operate for civilian traffic at the outbreak of the Second World War.

Black's *Guide to Kent*, written in 1882, describes Rye thus:

> A picturesque town with a curious mouldiness of antiquity about it, with streets where horses' hooves are not frequent enough to keep down the fast-climbing grass . . . Not an uninteresting town, for it belongs to an important chapter in English history, when the Cinque Ports were famous places, and their harbours were thronged with shipping, and their 'barons' were men of mark who doffed their caps to none . . .

Despite the somewhat unattractive image conjured up by this unflattering description, Rye has been fortunate in attracting a large number of historians and literary figures, particularly in the 19th and 20th centuries. William Holloway produced *The History and Antiquities of the Ancient Town and Port of Rye* in the last century, and was also responsible for the preservation of the town archives. Today the town is fortunate in possessing Leopold Amon Vidler's *New History of Rye*, first published in 1934. Written by a member of a family with long connections with the town, the book is a worthy successor to Holloway's great work. More recently, G. S. Bagley has produced *The Book of Rye*.

Many well-known writers have settled in and around Rye, including Henry James, the great American novelist, and E. F. Benson, both of whom lived at Lamb House. The latter, like so many inhabitants of Lamb House (including his own fictitious Lucia) became Mayor of Rye. Beatrix Potter used Rye as the background for her *Tale of the Faithful Dove* and in this century the novelist Rumer Godden lived for a time in Mermaid Street and used the town as a setting for her children's book *A Kindle of Kittens* (see *Rye Colour Guide*).

Since Van Dyck and Esselens visited Rye, many other artists have drawn inspiration from her charm. J. M. W. Turner painted several canvases in the district in the 18th century, and in the present century there were two conflicting groups of artists in the town; happily today both groups have merged to form the present flourishing club. Paul Nash, one of the most famous of modern English painters, lived for a time in Rye before the last war.

Today Rye can still boast a shipbuilding industry, albeit on a smaller scale than in the past. One of the early shipyards — Slade Yard — later became the site of Jempson's Haulage Contractors during the 1930s. Today this expanding business employs many local men. Other local enterprises have not been so fortunate, but Rye Harbour, which early in its history suffered from many problems, has now become the major site for a wide variety of operations.

The early years of the 20th century saw the opening of a Roman Catholic church; the building of a new grammar school; and the purchase of Battery House and Gun-garden by the Corporation. Rye Museum was formerly housed in Battery House, but has subsequently removed to the Ypres Tower, which during its long history has served many purposes, including those of gaol, mortuary and a private dwelling. Rye suffered from air attacks during both World Wars, particularly in the last war, when damage was sustained to many well-known buildings, including the Wesleyan chapel, the roof of the Ypres Tower, and the *Mermaid* Inn. Battery and Strand Houses were both completely destroyed.

With the passing of the Local Government Act of 1974, Rye lost her borough status and was amalgamated with Battle and Bexhill to form Rother District. However, the town has retained its mayoral office, and much of its traditional ceremony. Ceremonies associated with the Cinque Ports are still carried out, including the installation of the Lord Warden. In 1979 Queen Elizabeth the Queen Mother became the first woman to hold this office.

Rye has also preserved many of its old buildings. Even the streets are paved in cobbles, or, as they are known locally, 'boulders'. Newer properties have been sited on the out-skirts or approach roads to the town and where rebuilding has been carried out within the town proper it has been done in a sympathetic manner, a merging of new and old often featuring weather-boarding, a common building technique in the area from medieval times. Esther Meynell, writing in the *Sussex County Magazine* in 1934, said 'Rye may be seen, complete and perfect, like a vignette in some 14th-century Book of Hours' and this description still holds true today. As G. S. Bagley commented in *A Connoisseur's Guide to Rye* in 1979, the use of 'a wide variety of styles and tex-tures, not necessarily fine period examples, but everyday expediences, built by masons and carpenters for the small gentry, the professional and the tradesmen of an ancient town' have done much to preserve Rye's special charm.

Today Rye is a flourishing market town, supported by the fishing industry, boat building, light industries, and numerous potteries. The combination of the ancient past and the lively present blend harmoniously to enhance the appeal of this town, so much loved by visitors and tourists from all over the world.

2. The Common Seal of the Corporation of Rye; front and
obverse side. The ship shown on the seal is an early type with
an aft castle while the church is depicted in an unwalled town.
It is thought that this seal could date from the 13th century.

Local Landscapes and Buildings

3. (*above*) Looking towards Rye: a picture taken early this century.

4. (*left*) An engraving from J. M. W. Turner's painting 'A race against the tide' clearly demonstrates the artist's brilliant treatment of light. The town in the background is Rye and the structure to the right is Camber Castle. It also shows the flat marshy area (which was formerly Rye Bay) and the causeway which linked Rye and Winchelsea.

5. Shipyard Lane c.1880 looking towards Rye, before the development of South Undercliff. This photograph shows farm buildings near to the town.

6. (*above*) A painting of Rye town seen
from the river; this was a very popular
subject with many artists over the years.

7. Detail from an engraving showing Rye
by R. Brandard from a drawing by
W.H. Bartlett published in 1841.

8. (*left*) The Ypres Tower was built in the 13th century as part of the defences of Rye. It survived the sieges and sackings of Rye—which it was not strong enough to prevent—and was used as the town gaol in the last century. It was closed in 1891, and now houses Rye museum. Photograph no. 10 shows the pyramidal roof which was destroyed during a bomb attack in World War II. Steps lead down to the Gungarden, once used as a battery and later as a bowling green.

9. (*above*) Early this century the Battery Pleasure Grounds, or as they are more usually called the Gungarden, were opened to visitors. The field guns were purchased by public subscription in 1906. From this photograph (c.1910) it is easy to see the commanding position of Ypres Castle and the Battery overlooking the marshes.

10. (*left*) An early photograph of Rye Battery beside the Ypres Tower in 1858.

11. (*opposite page, above*) The Landgate from a copper engraving by J. Walker after a sketch by James Moore published in 1798.

12. (*opposite page, below*) The Landgate and forge c.1900. The Landgate, which dates from 1329, is the only survivor of three mighty portals which once guarded the town. It consists of a broad archway flanked by massive towers, with upper chambers. One arch is a pointed Gothic type, the other a less common elliptical one, although they are contemporaries. The clock was inserted as a memorial of the Prince Consort in 1863.

13. King Street, looking towards the Landgate, 1914. Miss Lilian Bryan and a small cousin are standing in the doorway of her toy shop, which is next door to the cycle and motor engineering business founded by her father.

14. King Street, looking northward about 1910; we can see the shop of Mr. E. Bryan, who is standing in his doorway below the sign advertising cars for hire.

15. Mermaid Street looking towards the Strand where one of the old gates of Rye (now demolished) originally stood. On the right is Hartshorne House, sometimes known as 'the Old Hospital', as it is said to have been used as such during the Napoleonic Wars. Samuel Jeake II acquired it as part of the dowry of his 13-year old wife Elizabeth Hartshorne when he married in 1680. This fine building of the 15th century was largely rebuilt at the end of the 16th century, but fell into disrepair during the 19th. Later it became the home of Rumer Godden, the novelist, who lived here during the 1960s.

16. The *Mermaid Inn* from a drawing by an unknown artist c.1920.

17. Rye High Street.

18. Rye High Street c.1910.

19. (*above*) Cinque Port Street, c.1905. The tobacconist E. E. Stocks also served teas and light refreshments while next door in The *King's Arms* Inn a stronger brew was offered by the proprietors C. Finn & Son. Originally called The *William IV*, it had ceased operating by 1910. During the mid-17th century Rye could boast of no less than 40 ale-house and inn keepers, and at that time certain of the landlords were accused of giving short measures.

20. (*below, left*) The street known as The Mint c.1900. During the 17th century there was a great shortage of small change and the tradesmen of Rye issued tokens of their own. The proprietors of both the *Ship* and the *Mermaid* inns issued farthing tokens, as did Thomas Boyce, a grocer. In 1668 the Corporation themselves issued a large number of farthings, but by 1672 these were ordered to be redeemed following the issue of a new regal farthing. The woman in this photograph is thought to be Mrs. Browning.

21. (*below right*) Watchbell Street, looking east, c.1900. In 1497 Adam Oxenbrege, the mayor, erected a bell to give warning of the coming of the French. This, combined with the Lookout at the end of the street facing towards Rye Bay, was considered adequate protection for the times.

22. Snow storm, Rye Hill, early this century.

23. An open air market on the steps of the Town Hall, before 1914. Early in its history, Market Street was called 'Boucherie' or 'Le Butcherie' and this name survived into the 18th century. The ground floor of the Town Hall was used as a market for meat, butter and other produce well into the middle of the 19th century. Before the construction of the new Town Hall this area was apparently most unpleasant with offal and stable clearings being thrown into the nearby churchyard.

24. The exact date of the foundation of the Augustinian priory is not known, but local records show it as being in existence by 1364. As it had a revenue of less than £200 per annum, it was one of the minor religious houses suppressed in 1535. Subsequently it was used for a variety of purposes. It is said that the French Huguenots who settled in Rye in the 16th century found refuge here. Later it became a theatre, malthouse, salt and provision store, wool warehouse, and during the First World War a hospital, before becoming a pottery. The old stone steps on the outside were erected at a time when the building was used for commercial purposes.

25.   The parish church of St Mary the Virgin, Rye, from a water-colour drawing by W.H. Borrow. This picture shows the pollarded trees and low picket fence lining the path. Although there is a tradition that an earlier church stood on this site there is no mention of it in Domesday Book. The building of the present church was started early in the 12th century when the town itself and much of the surrounding area was still held, under a royal deed of gift, by the Abbey of Fecamp in Normandy. It was built on the cruciform plan, with a long rectangular chancel and a central tower, but was not completed for over a hundred years when finally the two side chapels were added. Although the basic design has survived there have been many changes. The worst disaster in its history occurred in 1377 when Rye was looted and set on fire by French invaders and the church was extensively damaged. The tower collapsed, destroying some of the chancel, transept and north chapel arches, and much of the roof fell in. The church bells were taken to Normandy as booty, but the following year the men of Rye and Winchelsea recovered them. One of the bells was subsequently hung in Watchbell Street, to give warning of any future attack, and was not returned to the church until early in the 16th century. Repair of the building was a slow business but the tower was eventually rebuilt, though apparently on a less grand scale than before. At the Reformation much of the church's property in the way of land was sequestered and the interior stripped of its rood, images and ornaments. In 1701 the vicar and churchwardens petitioned the king for financial assistance, saying that the "church was so ruinous that people were afraid to attend services". It was not, however, until 1882 that a big restoration scheme was put in hand; the nave was reroofed, an entirely new clerestory constructed, the walls were strengthened, and the west door blocked up. This work was much criticised and it was said that the building had suffered more from this misguided zeal of the restorers than it had from the French and the Puritans during the previous centuries.

26.   (*opposite page*) Thomas House (left) is reputed to be one of the oldest buildings in West Street. A rendered facade often covers earlier timber-framed buildings. The house on the corner was once the property of Rye church. It was demolished in the latter part of the 19th century and a bank now occupies the site. This photograph was taken about 1890.

27. (*above*) The Garden Room at Lamb House where Henry James and then E. F. Benson lived for many years. In Benson's novels, Lucia and Mapp observed 'Tilling' (Rye) from the window of 'Mallards' (Lamb House). Henry James, who coveted Lamb House since he saw a sketch of the bow-windowed Garden Room, obtained a lease and later the freehold. It was here that he entertained many of his literary friends and wrote some of his best known books—he used Lamb House as a setting in *The Awkward Age*. Unfortunately the Garden Room was destroyed by a bomb during World War II.

28. E. F. Benson at Lamb House, 1930. This photograph was taken by Mr. Charles Tomlin, his man-servant for over twenty years. Mr. Benson shared the Welsh dog Taffy with its owner Rose, his cook who later became Mrs. Tomlin. Taffy is buried in the garden beneath a memorial stone.

29. The old Stone House, sometimes described as the Carmelite Friary. It is believed to have been a house of the short-lived Order of Friars Repentant of Jesus Christ, popularly known as the Friars of the Sack from their sack-cloth clothing. The House, founded in 1263, admitted married men and women who, because they were allowed to possess property, were not called friars but were deemed 'ecclesiastical persons'. This lack of strictness is thought to have caused their suppression in England in 1307. Later in its history the building became a private house, one of the oldest in the town.

30. The Quarter Boys following their restoration in 1902. It was at this time that the dial and Quarter Boys were re-painted and regilded by a local firm, G. Burnham & Son, at a cost of £11. This work was apparently carried out in honour of the coronation of Edward VII. Rumour had it that it was discovered that one of the figures was that of a girl, but this seems extremely unlikely!

31. This photograph (c.1900) shows the Town Hall. It was designed by Andrew Jelfe and built in 1741 of brick with Portland stone surrounds to the windows and arcades. The building was surmounted by a cupola wherein hung the Jurats' Bell used during quarter sessions. After a long absence this bell was replaced in 1981 to mark the wedding of Prince Charles and Lady Diana. From a Doric doorway a stair ascends to the court room, the walls of which are inscribed with the names of the mayors since 1289, the year of Rye's incorporation.

32. Old Ferry House, c.1900, where the ferryman, James Cook, lived in the last century.

33. Thatched cottage in Military Road. This type of roof is rarely seen in East Sussex and would most certainly have been banned in central Rye where fire risk was considerable due to the many timber-framed buildings.

34. (*opposite page*) A nostalgic photograph, taken about 1920, of Rye Mill on the River Tillingham. Unfortunately little documentary evidence on its history exists. It is thought that there may have been a mill on this site before 1850, and at one time the buildings here were used for storing grain. However, on 13 February 1930 the original main building was completely destroyed by fire. Rebuilding commenced almost immediately, but most of the internal mechanisms had been irreplaceably damaged. Today the mill exterior has been covered with a mixture of fibreglass and resin bonding.

35. (*right*) Cliff Cottage, Military Road, with the smock mill on the high ground behind. This picture is thought to date from 1862; the mill was demolished about 1884.

36. Rye Swing Bridge, erected on the Ashford, Rye and Hastings branch of the South-Eastern Railway where the line crosses the River Rother. Its total weight was 116 tons and its length 112 feet. The bridge could be swung open to enable the passage of those ships unable to lower their masts. The swinging of the bridge was accomplished by means of spur and bevil-wheels and it took two men about two and a half minutes to complete the operation. The bridge was demolished in 1903 and replaced by a double track fixed span bridge.

Shipping

37. (*left*) The building with the very pronounced crooked chimney is the old Customs House, built in the 15th century. Tradition claims that Queen Elizabeth I on her visit to Rye in 1573 was entertained here when it was then called 'Grene Hall'. Note the cobbled street, a familiar feature in the town.

38. (*below*) Notice of a sale of seized goods. This appeared in the *Sussex Weekly Advertiser: Or, Lewes Journal* of 9 April 1781 and gives some idea of the extent of the smuggling which was carried out in the area at that time.

39. (*opposite page, above*) Boats moored in Rye Harbour looking towards the town of Rye seen in the distance.

40. (*opposite page, below*) James Cook, ferryman at Rye in the last century. For many years he lived in the small ferry cottage where he and his wife Harriet raised a large family: they had 22 children, including two sets of twins who died in infancy. This photograph was taken about 1880.

This is to give NOTICE, THAT at the CUSTOM-HOUSE, on Thursday the 19th Day of April next, at Ten of the Clock in the Forenoon, there will be put up to Sale for Home Consumption, in sundry Lots,

950 Gallons of Brandy,
273 Gallons of Geneva,
1352 Pounds of Black Tea,
4333 Pounds of Wool,
A VESSEL and Furniture.

The Goods to be viewed the Day before, and Morning of the Sale.

N. B. 25*l.* per Cent. will be required as a Deposite,

RYE, March 27, 1781.

41. At one time this anchor, dredged up in Rye Bay, was a popular exhibit in the Gungarden. It is seen here with Mr. Cryer, who was responsible for locking the garden at night. He was apparently a great favourite with the many children thereabouts despite his semi-official status. This photograph dates from c.1909.

42. Early this century boat trips along the River Rother were a popular form of amusement. This picture (c.1910) would seem to have been taken at the beginning of the season as neither of the vessels has its sun awning erected.

43. Strand Quay at floodtide c.1960. The warehouses seen on the left of the photograph stand on the original quayside of the Middle Ages and were used for a variety of purposes, particularly during the 19th century when Rye was a busy port with many boat-builders' yards alongside the river. It has been claimed that Rye was the birthplace of the English navy at the time of King Alfred but there is no evidence to substantiate this.

44.   Strand Quay c.1890. During the 16th century the principal market was on the Strand and in 1556 store-houses and a crane were erected.

45. (*opposite page*) The Quay early this century. The large house on the left of the picture was destroyed by enemy bombs during World War II.

46. (*above*) and 47. (*below*) Records show that ships were built and repaired at Rye as early as the 13th century. The middle years of the 19th century were however the 'golden age' when there were three yards operating, Hessle and Holmes and Hoad Bros. being two of the biggest. The Strand and Rock Channel were the main shipbuilding areas and over forty vessels were launched during the first decade of this century. Prior to World War I Rye shipbuilders specialised in sailing trawlers of the ketch type.

Earning A Living

48. This photograph, taken about 1900, records the last sail-maker at work in Britt's loft, a large room where the sails were cut out and made. This was very heavy work which gradually ceased as boat-building in the town declined.

49. (*right*) This photograph, c.1900, shows fishermen at Camber near Rye engaged in keddle, or 'kettle', net fishing. The nets were strung between stakes driven into the sand and as the sea receded the fishermen scooped the stranded fish, mainly mackerel, into a horse-drawn cart.

50. (*left*) The small gaff-rigged boats of Rye harbour used to sail to the surrounding beaches where they collected the unique blue flints, known locally as 'boulders', which were then sent to the Staffordshire potteries. This work was extremely badly paid. This picture (c.1920) shows the unloading of the boulder boats which was done by hand.

51. (*right*) Rother Ironworks, Fishmarket Road, viewed from the river, c.1880.

52. (*left*) Rye was strategically placed to have its own brewery as it was a collection and distribution centre for hops. At one time East Guldeford Brewery was owned by the well-known Lamb family but later it passed into the possession of Messrs. Chapman Bros. The brewery was wood-fired and the fuel used may be seen to the right of the picture.

53. and 54. (*below, left and right*) The demolition of East Guldeford Brewery in 1911.

THE PULLING DOWN OF EAST GULEFORD BREWERY SHAFT JULY 11. 1911. THE FALLING SHAFT

55. Hop pickers in the vicinity of Rye in the early years of this century. Many families from the East End of London came annually during the hop picking season, but it is thought that these pickers were local people.

56. Haymaking c.1900, a once familiar sight on the farms surrounding Rye.

57. (*left*) Mr. Simpson (later of Jenner & Simpson) and Edgar L. Stoneham, agricultural merchants, outside their office on the Strand. Note the building which is of weatherboarding, and the lamp which is particularly attractive.

58. (*below*) Mr. William Henry Axell was the founder of this Hygienic Laundry. At this time, 1919, many laundries made a point of stressing the word 'hygienic' whilst others preferred to advertise their 'own drying grounds'. Mr. Axell, the only son of a trawler skipper operating out of Rye, had ten sisters and it is interesting to speculate whether any of them helped in the laundry. It was due to his father-in-law, Mr. Edward Bryan, that the laundry cart, originally a horse-drawn vehicle, was upgraded to a motor van within the space of two years.

59. (*opposite page*) Washerwoman at work in Mermaid Passage c.1890. It is thought that at least half-a-dozen women practised this trade here in the latter part of the last century.

60. Members of Rye police force outside the police station in Church Square, 1911. P.C. Muggridge (centre back row) later moved to Winchelsea where he served during World War I, being responsible for finding local billets for troops stationed there. From left to right standing: P.C. Ber P.C. Muggridge, P.C. Boniface; seated: Supe intendent Whitlock and P. C. Sinclair.

61. The pillory and gibbet chains with the skull of a man called Breads are on view in the Town Hall. In 1743 Breads, who owned the *Flushing Inn* and a butcher's shop, was fined by the magistrate James Lamb for giving short weight. Breads threatened to get even with him and was later seen drunk, shouting 'Butchers should kill Lambs'. Lamb's brother-in-law, Allen Grebell, borrowed Lamb's cloak and went in his place to have dinner with a nephew on board a ship moored off the Fishmarket. On his way home through the churchyard Grebell was stabbed by Breads who had mistaken him for Lamb. Although Grebell, thinking that a drunk had collided with him, managed to reach home, he was found dead the next morning having bled to death. Breads was hanged on the Salts and his body was chained to a gibbet. The ghosts of both Allen Grebell and his murderer are reputed to have been seen at different times in the churchyard.

62. The fire brigade passing through the narrow streets of Rye. This picture was probably taken at the time of the coronation of Edward VII. This engine was hand operated; motorised ones were introduced in 1903 and by 1910 were in general use. The driver of the fire engine was an employee of Wright and Pankhurst, furniture removers of Tower Street where the horses were also stabled.

63. Rye fire brigade about 1900 when it was commanded by Captain Gasson. With so many timbered buildings in the town fire was always a grave risk.

64. This Rye fire engine, dated 1745, is now on display in the museum. It is a "box type" and although it has four wooden solid wheels it was normally conveyed to the fire on a horse-drawn wagon.

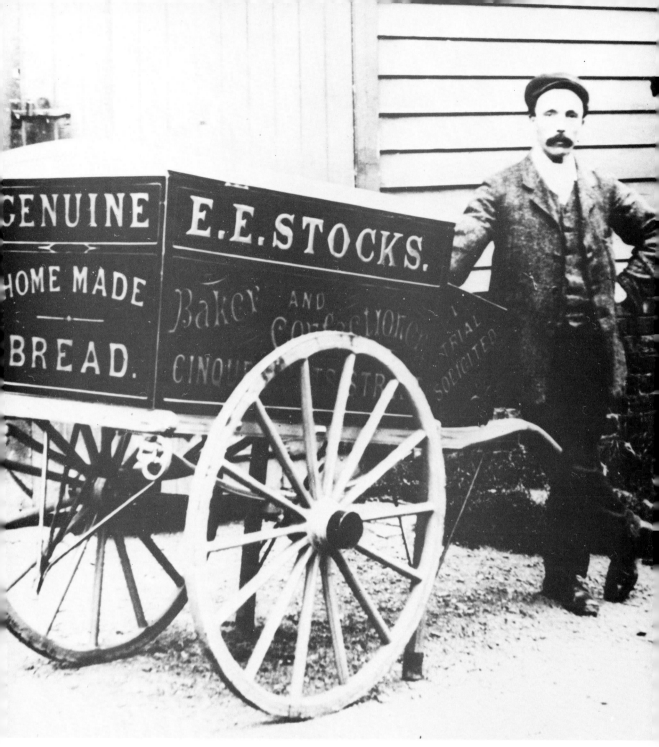

65.   Baker's van belonging to E. E. Stocks. Unfortunately it has been impossible to identify the delivery man.

66. Mr. Clark outside his shop at 32 Ferry Road c.1910. The window appears to be well stocked with a wide selection of merchandise, including a number of bottles. Handcarts were popular with tradesmen for transporting goods, particularly as delivery of merchandise was a service many of them offered.

67. (*left*) Mr. and Mrs. Dunk standing outside their shop in Mint Street, c.1930. Previously this shop had been owned by Mr. C. Ellis, a baker whose business card stated that 'fancy bread and biscuit' were a speciality of his shop. He also sold toys —a strange combination of commodities!

68. (*opposite page*) Deacon's Printing Works, the depot for Rye Pottery and Lending Library, c.1900. Deacon's printed an illustrated guide to Rye and handsomely bound books with the crest of the Cinque Ports on the cover. The reverse side of this postcard advertises Deacon's Library and Steam Printing Works and since there is only sufficient room for the address to be written one wonders if this is an early and cheap form of advertising.

69. In 1853 Isaac Parsons, formerly of Beckley, set up a small printing press in the garden shed of his home in Rye and began producing a small four-page newspaper called *The South Eastern Advertiser*. Later in life he branched out as a printer, stationer and bookseller, and produced the newspaper *The Rye Chronicle*. This photograph shows Isaac Parsons outside his office. It is thought that one of the boys seen here may have been his son who moved to Hastings and started *The Hastings Observer*.

70. (*right*) Mr. E. Bryan outside the cycle shop he founded in the latter part of the last century. He originally made custom-built bicycles but early in the motoring boom he opened a garage, engineering works and car hire firm. This photograph was taken about 1895.

71. (*below*) This photograph taken c.1908 shows the two youngest children of Mr. E. Bryan, Lilian and William, with cycles built in their father's workshop.

Transport

72. Mr. E. Bryan is seen here with his fleet of cars. For many years his garage in Fishmarket Road was called 'Bryan's Corner' and it was marked as such on some local street maps.

73. An early motor accident at Rye Hill showing the badly damaged vehicle and two interested young spectators.

74. The *Camber* c.1912. Always known as the Rye and Camber tramway this single 3-ft. gauge ran for 1¾ miles, from the terminus at the south-east corner of the Monkbretton bridge to Rye Harbour village. The line was opened on 13 July 1895, extended to Camber Sands on 13 July 1908 and finally closed for civilian use in 1939, though it continued to be used for various duties in connection with the Admiralty. On the first Bank Holiday that the railway was in operation receipts amounted to £12 5s., and during the first month after opening 18,000 tickets were sold. A first class single cost 4d. and a return 6d. while a second class single cost 2d., return 4d. Fishermen usually bought an annual season ticket for £1 10s. which could be used by a whole boat crew.

75. This photograph taken about 1910 shows the steam rail-car which used to operate six times daily between Hastings and Rye.

STEAM
Communication
WITH
BOULOGNE.

THAT FAST, COMMODIOUS, SEA-GOING VESSEL,

The **WINDSOR CASTLE**, John Murray, **Commander,**
OR
The **EDINBURGH CASTLE**, W. Barry, **Commander,**
WILL

Leave RYE for BOULOGNE
On SATURDAY, the 25th INST.
AT 8 O'CLOCK IN THE MORNING,
And continue running, according to the time of Tide, every

WEDNESDAY & SATURDAY,
Returning the following THURSDAY and MONDAY,
UNTIL FURTHER NOTICE.

FARES: TO BOULOGNE, 7s. 6d. and 5s.; FROM BOULOGNE, 5s.
CARRIAGES, 2 Guineas. HORSES, 1 Guinea.

These splendid Vessels, unequalled on the Coast for Accommodation, have lately undergone most extensive Repairs in their Engines; rendering them, in every respect, a very desirable medium of Communication.

The greatest punctuality will be observed in starting, and every regulation used to ensure comfort and safety to the Passengers.

Messrs. ALLEN & FOWLE, Rye, AGENTS,
UNDER THE SUPERINTENDENCE OF A COMMITTEE.

RYE, 14th May, 1839. (TAYLOR, PRINTER.)

76. The shortest route across the Channel to France in 1839 was by a fast and commodious sea-going steam vessel which sailed from Rye to Boulogne. At least, such was the claim of those who operated the service which ran every Wednesday and Saturday, returning the following Thursday and Monday (weather permitting), at a cost of 7s. 6d. and 5s. single fares. Apparently the service was mainly used for business and holidays on the continent.

Schools

77.   The Mixed Infant School in Lion Street 1911. The seven-year-old girl holding the slate is Margaret Muggridge, daughter of a local police constable (see Pl.60). She described her school days as 'very strict; we had to sit up straight with our arms behind our backs unless writing. Once a week we did clay modelling. The clay was sticky stuff like putty, and after using it we had to line up to wash our hands as there was only one basin and no hot water'. At this time the headmistress was Miss Gamble who by all accounts was a martinet.

78.   Nature study class enjoying a practical lesson in the open air. It is interesting to see these children of the Edwardian age with their heavy boots studded with metal, gaiters, and a wide variety of headgear.

79. Rye Grammar School c.1890.
The brick building is modelled on
classical lines. It was erected in 1636
and is one of the earliest examples
in England of the 'giant order' of
pilasters which extend through two
storeys. Thomas Peacocke, Jurat of
Rye, left an endowment 'to educate
the poor boys of Rye'. It was a
model for W. M. Thackeray in his
unfinished novel *Denis Duval*:
'I was sent to a famous good school,
Pocock's Grammar School at Rye,
where I learned to speak English
like a Briton born as I am, and not
as we did at home... At Pocock's
I got a little smattering of Latin too,
and plenty of fighting for the first
month or two'.

80. The senior boys' classroom at the Grammar School c.1905. At this time Peacock's School consisted of two
classrooms. The fees were £1 10s. to £1 15s. per term for day pupils whilst boarding fees ranged from nine to
eleven guineas; free stationery was provided together with books and laundry. The boys were encouraged to take
an active part in outside activities, sport and gymnastics.

81. Boys from the Grammar School giving a display of physical exercises on the Town Salts recreation ground.
Other young people celebrated the coronation of Edward VII with flag drills, marching and dancing displays.

Occasions and Personalities

82. Local children dancing around the maypole on
the Town Salts. In the early years of this century
the Mayday celebrations were a popular event in
the children's lives. A large crowd of interested by-
standers are observing this dance.

83. Rye Regatta 1902. The man standing on the bow sprit could be a local person called Johnny Milgate who was a fine swimmer. Presumably he was attempting to negotiate the slippery pole, an event popular with the spectators. Many decorated boats of all types took part in the proceedings and other events taking place included sailing races and the rowing match between four-oared galleys which was always watched with keen interest.

84. Dancing bear in Mermaid Street, c.1910. This animal was a great favourite with all the children when it performed in the town. Its owner lodged overnight at the now defunct *Jolly Sailor* inn and the bear was caged in a heavily barred shed.

85. Cinque Port Volunteer Band c.1900. Frederick William Bryan, the conductor, (seated fifth from right, second row) made the copper-plated instrument, which could be a dulcimer, seen in the centre of the photograph.

86. Buglers greeting the morning of George V's coronation from the top of Rye church, 1910. Unfortunately it has been impossible to identify any of these young men but they may be members of the Cinque Port Territorial Band.

87. (*above*) Rye decorated for the coronation of Edward VII in 1902. This photograph shows Mr. Dunk outside his shop in the High Street.

88. (*opposite page, above*) This photograph, taken in 1902, shows some of the many local children who took part in the festivities marking Edward VII's coronation. These celebrations had been postponed due to the King's attack of appendicitis and subsequent operation. Note the women wearing bonnets in the style of the late Queen Victoria.

89. (*opposite page, below*) An interdenominational memorial service was held in honour of King Edward VII in St Mary's church. Members from all local services took part and this picture shows the officers and men of Rye fire brigade about to enter the church.

MEMORIAL
SERVICE AT RYE
TO KING EDWARD VII

90. (*left*) The coronation procession for King George V parading through the streets of Rye. It is thought that the uniformed figure on horseback leading the parade may be Colonel Butterfield.

91. (*below*) This photograph taken in 1910 shows the proclamation of the ascension of King George V being read by the Mayor of Rye, at that time Councillor J. Adams, from the steps of the Town Hall. Note the two mace-bearers carrying their badge of office and wearing top hats; today hats are not worn.

92. (*above*) Sunday school children queuing to collect their Jubilee mugs during the celebrations commemorating 25 glorious years of the reign of King George V and Queen Mary, 1935.

93. (*right*) Councillor H. O. Schofield, Mayor 1949-50, scattering hot pennies to the crowd on the occasion of the mayor-making. This tradition seems to be rooted in mystery and various theories on its origin have been put forward, including the unlikely one that an early mayor called for pennies to 'reward' the crowd and as there were none available newly minted ones hot from the mint were used. During the latter part of the last century this action was particularly popular with not only the local children but also the sailors.

94. (*above*) Captain Alexander Vidler and Mrs. Vidler c.1865. He is attired in the officers' tunic of the Cinque Ports Artillery Volunteers which was completed by a pill-box cap.

95. (*opposite page*) Mace-bearers holding the two maces, originally those of the Mayor and the King's Bailiff. The town of Rye was a royal manor before it was incorporated as a royal borough in 1289 and got its first Mayor. The Bailiff and the Mayor each had their own mace but by 1700 these offices were combined. The two smaller maces on display are 16th-century and the larger date from the late 1760s. The flag is that of the Cinque Ports.

96. (*left*) The photograph shows the magnificently decorated capital E from a transcript of Queen Elizabeth I's *inspeximus* of the Cinque Ports' charters, dated 8 March 1560.

97. (*below*) Proclamation relating to the visit of Queen Elizabeth I in August 1573. At that time she was 39 years of age and had been on the throne of England 15 years. The whole 'Cinque Port Tour' of the Queen and her entourage lasted some ten weeks. The Queen took a keen interest in the defence of the town, visiting the Gungarden before touring the Fishmarket and boatyards. On leaving Rye she is said to have dubbed the town 'Rye Royal' in celebration of this happy visit, the culmination of which was a presentation to her by the mayor of a purse of 100 gold angels (coins of the time). It has subsequently been discovered that the mayor had had to borrow this money.

98. (*opposite page, above*) Queen Mary, consort to King George V, on a semi-private visit to Rye in 1935. The Queen, an avid collector of antiques, was said to enjoy her visit to the antique shops in the town. At this time the King was convalescing at Compton Place, Eastbourne, a few miles along the coast. The building in the background was bombed during World War II. From left to right: Canon Fowler, Queen Mary, Aubrey Smith, Pip Meade and Sir Brian Godfrey Foussett, an equerry.

99. (*opposite page, below*) The Queen Mother signing the visitors' book in Market Place under the Town Hall. The Mayor of Rye, Mrs. Jo Kirkham, is on her left and behind is her daughter Tracy, who at 13 was the youngest Mayoress in England when appointed in May 1979. The Queen Mother came to the town on 9 July 1980 in her capacity as Lord Warden of the Cinque Ports, and to view the cannon made especially to re-arm the Gungarden in honour of her 80th birthday.

The first anointed Queene I am:
Within this town which euer came.

¶A saying of each good Subiect of Rye.

Happy town, O happy Rye:
that once in thee y Queen doth ly
Such ioy before was neuer seen
In Rye as now to lodge the Queen.
You fisher men of Rye reioyce:
To see your Queen & hear her voice.
Now clap your hands reioice & sing:
which neuer erst lodged Queen ne king.
Reioyce thou town and porte of Rye:
To see thy souerains Meiestie.
What hart hath he that dwelles in Rye:
That ioyes not now as wel as I:
Oh God that giuest life and breth:
Preserue our Queen Elizabeth.

Viuat Nestorios Elizabetha dies.

From a map of Sussex by John Norden, augmented by John Speede.
a 1616 d.

100.   An early map of Hastings Rape. Camber Castle may be seen on the spit of land guarding the entrance to both Rye and Winchelsea. Old Winchelsea lies to the south of the coast but the exact site is unknown.

Winchelsea

WINCHELSEA – INTRODUCTION

WINCHELSEA HAS HAD A LONG and varied history. The present town (or rather, the remaining fragment) is not the original Winchelsea. As early as 959 there was a mint here, but whether the town existed before the Roman conquest of Britain is a matter of doubt. Its name is from the Old English word *wincelesea* or *winceleseg*, meaning 'an island', or 'water in an angle of land'.

In 1031 King Canute granted the manor of Ramslie and its port, Old Winchelsea, to the Norman abbey of Fecamp, which was under the patronage of the Dukes of Normandy. This grant was of crucial importance in the history of England. It gave the Normans a foothold on a very vulnerable part of the coast; it is possible that without the possession of Ramslie, Duke William's invasion of England would have failed, and the future history not only of England but of Western Europe would have been very different.

Winchelsea was already a port of considerable importance in the 11th century, and its loyalty to its Norman overlords brought it further prosperity. However, its successful life was to be cut short by the inroads of the sea in the 13th century. As early as 1236 the town had petitioned the King for help, as the shingle spit on which it stood was being eroded away by the sea. In 1250 it was partially submerged by a phenomenally high tide, which 'flowed twice without ebbing with a horrible roaring and a glint as of a fire on the waves'. Subsequently, many of Winchelsea's inhabitants deserted it.

The decline of the port was further hastened in 1266, when Prince Edward attacked the town, took it by storm, and put all the principal inhabitants to the sword. He took this extreme course of action because the seamen, described as little better than pirates, who sailed out of Winchelsea preyed on friend and foe alike. By the time Edward ascended the throne in 1272 the town was gradually falling into decay, although its port was still much frequented.

In 1282 a Commission was sent to examine the situation. Following its report, King Edward I acted rapidly. A new site (on the Hill of Iham, a name later corrupted to 'Higham') was selected for the town. Plans were drawn up, and it is believed that the town was designed by the King on the gridiron principle, already adopted for towns in his domain of Aquitaine. His decision was none too soon. After the great storm of 1287 no trace of the old town remained.

The site selected for the new town was on a peninsula rising above the low-lying surrounding countryside. Its northern cliff was washed by the River Brede, which was wider than it is today, and had good access to the sea. Within the squares formed by the streets which were laid out to cross each other at right angles, suitable plots were demarcated for each householder by name. It is still possible today to draw up a plan of the town as originally laid out from the Rent Roll of 1292. The Hill of Iham had been inhabited from ancient times, and its church of St Leonard may date from pre-Conquest days. Old Winchelsea is thought to have had about 700 households, and thus a population of around 3,000-4,000 persons. By the end of the 14th century New

Winchelsea may have had a similar population, spaciously settled around 39 great squares, intercepted by seven roads. The streets running east and west were known as 'First', 'Second' and 'Third' Streets, as in an American town today.

The harbour was on the River Brede, therefore it was a river and not a seaport. It was tidal; ships entered at high tide and were beached as the water ebbed. The public quay was to be found at the bottom of Strand Hill, and it was probably from here that, as W. MacLean Homan suggests in *A Short Account of the History and Antiquities of Winchelsea* (1936), Winchelsea ships carried 15th-century pilgrims to the shrine of St James of Compostella in Spain.

It is believed that the town was governed by a mayor chosen by the townspeople from about 1290 onwards, who chose 12 'jurats' to assist him. These worthy citizens had considerable privileges at the time; today a mayor and jurats are still appointed every Easter Monday, but they no longer have their special rights. The Crown was represented by the King's Bailiff, who shared supreme authority with the mayor.

In 1315 Winchelsea was admitted as a full corporate member of the Cinque Ports Confederation. The Cinque Ports levy of ships was generally 57, of which Winchelsea provided 10, a clear indication of the town's size and importance. On several occasions Winchelsea men were in charge of the whole fleet; the first of these was Gervase Alard, who appears to have had command between 1300 and 1307. In 1415 King Henry V's flagship, the *Gabrielle de Winchelsea*, was built in Winchelsea, although the fleet sailed for France from Portchester.

The market square was situated to the south-west of the present Grey Friars House, but all traces of buildings in this area have disappeared. The Town Hall may have stood on the east side, and near it were probably the Bailiff's Court Hall and the prison, over which the Bailiff had control. The building known today as the Court Hall, where the mayoral election takes place, possibly formed part of the house of Reginald Alard, who had acquired the site when the town was first built in the 13th century. It is believed that many leading citizens of medieval Winchelsea owned three properties; one at the harbour near their ships, one residential property near St Thomas's church; and a third near the market square normally used for the storage of imported goods and for manufacturing.

The town was essentially devoted to manufactures and to trade, mainly with Flanders and Gascony, but there is evidence of commercial relations with other more distant places, including Portugal, Italy and the Baltic ports. The port was primarily used for the exporting of a considerable quantity of ale and beer, and several breweries and beer houses were sited near the quay. Gascon wine was one of the main imports, and the magnificent vaulted cellars still to be found under many of the buildings obviously date from the foundation of the town and were used for the storage of wine. Unfortunately no evidence of the trade guilds which undoubtedly existed at this time remains, but it is known that a curious system of communal trading operated.

Winchelsea was a walled town, approached by at least four gates. Today three of them still remain. One of them — Strand Gate — is the original gate, and leads to the harbour. The Pipewell or Land Gate leading to Rye, via Udimore, was destroyed during the French occupation of 1380, but it was rebuilt by John Helde, Mayor of Winchelsea in 1404-5. The third entrance was the New Gate, sited some distance from the town on the road to Pett and Fairlight. It was through this gate that the French entered when they sacked Winchelsea in 1380. Tradition has it that it was opened to them by treachery. During the last years of the 14th century, due to the declining population, the town applied for and received permission to reduce its total size and to erect new walls, but this work appears to have been abandoned about 1415. This may have been due to further French raids after the battle of Agincourt, when the French held the Channel, but no clear evidence of this has been found.

There were two churches within the town, St Thomas, and St Giles. The original parish church, St Leonard's, stood outside the town and was considerably older. It belonged to the Abbot of Fecamp until 1414, when foreign monasteries were no longer permitted to own properties in England. This church fell into ruin during the 15th century, and St Giles was also to fall into disuse in the next century. Recently the latter has been the subject of archaeological investigation. The present parish church (St Thomas's) was dedicated to St Thomas à Becket and was founded during the 13th century. The choir appears to have been completed about 1312. However, the church suffered badly from French attacks on the town during the next two centuries. In 1380 it was the turn of the Castilian fleet of Admiral Sanches de Tover to 'terrorise the Thames and fire Winchelsea and the approaches of London'. It is thought to have been on this occasion when the nave of the church was burnt to the ground. The 17th-century diarist, John Evelyn, wrote a vivid description of the 'forlorn ruins' which he found at Winchelsea.

There were also two friaries in the town. The Grey Friars were already in occupation when the new town of Winchelsea moved to Iham. Their friary was large and handsome, and for upwards of 300 years it continued to flourish. At the Dissolution King Henry VIII put it into the hands of George Clyfford and Michael Welbore, who preserved a large portion of the fabric by using the house as a farmhouse and the chapel as a barn. In 1819 the property came into the possession of Richard Stileman, who demolished the old house and used the materials from it to build a new one. All that remains today of the original structure is the ruined chancel. Both W. M. Thackeray and Henry James found inspiration for their work in 'The Friars'.

The other group of friars who settled in Winchelsea during the Middle Ages were the Black Friars. At first the townspeople made a great effort to keep them out, but in 1359 King Edward III granted them a site within the town walls. This friary too was abolished with the Dissolution of the Monasteries, and no effort seems to have been made to preserve the building. Material from it may have been used in the construction of Camber Castle in 1539.

Winchelsea could boast three hospitals or almshouses. These were not under the control of the church, but had secular priors and prioresses to run them. The 'brothers' and 'sisters' who found homes in St John's and St Bartholomew's (the latter was also known as 'Our Lady of Nazareth') were selected by the mayor and the jurats from amongst the 'deserving poor' of the town. Little is known of the history of the third institution, the Holy Cross.

By the time of the Spanish Armada, Winchelsea had declined so much that it did not possess a single vessel. When Queen Elizabeth I visited the town in 1573, the citizens petitioned her for a grant to help pay for works to keep the harbour open, which by that time had become almost entirely unserviceable. The Queen answered them courteously, ironically referring to the semi-derelict port as 'Little London', but no grant was forthcoming. Within a year or two of her visit, one contemporary observer declared that there were not above 60 households left. Sir Walter Raleigh commented that 'There be many havens which have been famous and now are gone to decay as Winchelsea'.

Some slight revival of the town economy took place in the 16th and 17th centuries when French refugees brought their weaving skills to Winchelsea. They used the stone vaults for their business. Later, in addition to cultivating flax and weaving linen, cambric and lawn were also manufactured. However, owing to more successful competition from elsewhere in the country, by 1810 the remaining weavers removed to Norwich, by then a centre of the textile manufacturing industry.

By the 18th century the once-great Winchelsea fair held on 14 May had dwindled to a small local affair of pedlars and gingerbread, and the weekly Saturday market was almost disused. Tanning was one of the last industries to be carried on in the town, but by the early years of the next century the tan yards were disused.

During these troubled times Winchelsea was often frequented by smugglers, who no doubt found the old wine vaults very convenient for their purposes. In 1770 the Supervisor of Customs in the town reported that only two dragoons were quartered there to assist the officers of the Customs and Excise and 'it frequently happens that the officers of both revenues want their assistance at the same time'. As 'very large gangs of smugglers often assemble on the coasts of that district', three more dragoons with horses were requested. We do not know, however, if his pleas were answered. (For further information, see Kenneth M. Clark, *Smuggling in Rye and District*, 1977.)

John Wesley came to Winchelsea and preached one of his last outdoor sermons under what was to become known as 'Wesley's Tree'; he apparently had more success here than in the neighbouring town of Rye. The record of the visit he made in his *Diary* runs:

> I went over to that poor skeleton of ancient Winchelsea ... I stood under a large tree ... and called to most of the inhabitants of the town: 'the Kingdom of Heaven is at hand; repent and believe the Gospel'. It seemed as if all that heard were, at the present, almost persuaded to be Christians.

Less than six months after this visit the great apostle of the 18th century was in his grave.

During the Napoleonic Wars troops were stationed in the town, and Bear Square was renamed Barrack Square. The men were quartered in a long building which is still standing today, divided into cottages. Turner commemorated this occasion in his painting of 'Soldiers at the Foot of Strand Hill', and also recorded the New Gate in 'Liber Studiorum'. He also painted the Military Road in the picture called 'A Race Against the Tide'. This road, badly built on a shifting foundation, connected Winchelsea with Rye and Appledore. A military canal built at the same time was intended as a means of moving men and materials should the French invade. It runs from Cliff End past Winchelsea, Rye and Appledore to terminate at Hythe in Kent.

From the reign of Edward III until the passing of the Reform Act of 1832, Winchelsea possessed the privilege of returning two members of parliament. It was greatly to the credit of Winchelsea's two last M.P.s, James Brougham and Judge Williams, that they voted for reform and thus for the abolition of the 'rotten borough' which they themselves represented. After 1832 Winchelsea became one of the electoral parishes tacked on to the borough of Rye. Later a Royal Commission investigated the unreformed corporations of the kingdom, and recommended the abolition of all of these, including Winchelsea. The town lost its magisterial and other functions, but its corporation was eventually allowed to remain in existence for the annual payment of a sum of less than £20 derived from the town's rents and King's dues. The mayor and jurats continued to exist to carry out this work through a Hundred Court.

While Daniel Defoe described Winchelsea in its decline as 'a skeleton of an ancient city rather than a real town', other men of genius found much to attract them. W. M. Thackeray stayed there whilst working on his novel *Denis Duval*, and other visitors included John Ruskin and Ford Madox Ford. Sir John Millais painted two pictures using the church of St Thomas as a setting. Ellen Terry the actress lived there, and was frequently visited by Sir Henry Irving and other friends from the world of the theatre. Henry James, who settled in the nearby town of Rye described the view from Winchelsea Look-Out at sunset:

> The best hour is that at which the compact little pyramid of Rye, crowned by its big but stunted church, and quite covered by the westering sun, gives out the full measure of its old browns that turn to red, and its old reds, that turn to purple.

Medieval Winchelsea was no ordinary town; its large size, the scale and magnificence of its public buildings, and the fine craftsmanship apparent in the surviving parts of remaining domestic buildings, all clearly show that it was meant to be an English town worthy of its function expressed in a contemporary document as 'a key, refuge and guard of these parts against the tempestuousness of the sea and the insults of our enemies' (*see* Peter Brandon, *The Sussex Landscape*, 1974, pp. 219–220). While the town almost from its inception failed to develop as its creators had hoped, nevertheless it is of great historical interest, and few visitors can fail to appreciate its quiet charm and restful atmosphere.

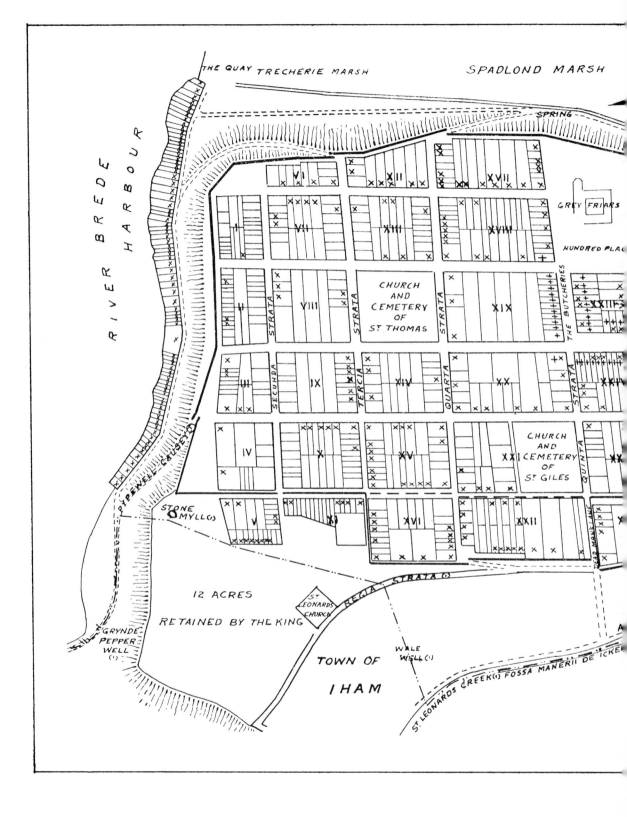

101. Plan of Winchelsea as originally laid out, reconstructed from the rent roll of 1292.

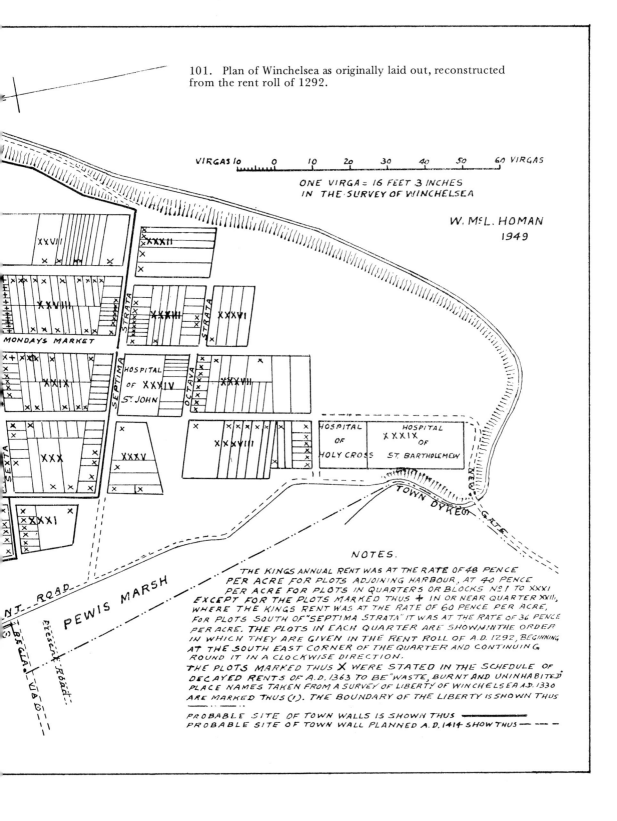

VIRGAS 10   0   10   20   30   40   50   60 VIRGAS

ONE VIRGA = 16 FEET 3 INCHES
IN THE·SURVEY OF WINCHELSEA

W. McL. HOMAN
1949

XXVII

XXXII

XXVIII

STRATA   STRATA

XXXVII   XXXVI

MONDAYS MARKET

SEPTIMA STRATA

HOSPITAL
OF XXXIV
St. JOHN

OCTAVA

XXXVIII

XXIX

SEXTA

XXX   XXXV

XXXVIII

HOSPITAL
OF
HOLY CROSS

HOSPITAL
XXXIX OF
St. BARTHOLEMEW

NEW GATE

XXXI

TOWN DYKE

NT. ROAD   PEWIS MARSH

BECLIA WAO

Crescent Road

NOTES.

THE KINGS ANNUAL RENT WAS AT THE RATE OF 48 PENCE
PER ACRE FOR PLOTS ADJOINING HARBOUR, AT 40 PENCE
PER ACRE FOR PLOTS IN QUARTERS OR BLOCKS No I TO XXXI
EXCEPT FOR THE PLOTS MARKED THUS + IN OR NEAR QUARTER XXIII,
WHERE THE KINGS RENT WAS AT THE RATE OF 60 PENCE PER ACRE,
FOR PLOTS SOUTH OF "SEPTIMA STRATA" IT WAS AT THE RATE OF 36 PENCE
PER ACRE. THE PLOTS IN EACH QUARTER ARE SHOWN IN THE ORDER
IN WHICH THEY ARE GIVEN IN THE RENT ROLL OF A.D. 1292, BEGINNING
AT THE SOUTH EAST CORNER OF THE QUARTER AND CONTINUING
ROUND IT IN A CLOCKWISE DIRECTION.
THE PLOTS MARKED THUS X WERE STATED IN THE SCHEDULE OF
DECAYED RENTS OF A.D. 1363 TO BE "WASTE, BURNT AND UNINHABITED"
PLACE NAMES TAKEN FROM A SURVEY OF LIBERTY OF WINCHELSEA A.D. 1330
ARE MARKED THUS (1). THE BOUNDARY OF THE LIBERTY IS SHOWN THUS

PROBABLE SITE OF TOWN WALLS IS SHOWN THUS ━━━━━
PROBABLE SITE OF TOWN WALL PLANNED A.D. 1414 SHOW THUS ━ ─── ─

102. (left) The ancient Seal of the Corporation of Winchelsea which dates from the early part of the reign of Edward I. The obverse side shows a ship with a poop and embattled forecastle. It has a crew of eight men. One of them is steering and the two above his head have immense speaking-trumpets, similar to those seen in many seals of the period. Four of the crew are engaged in drawing in a cable and squaring a yard, whilst the remaining man is ascending the backstay. A star and crescent are seen above the yard and beneath it is the royal arms of three lions passant. The translation of the motto reads 'The Seal of the Barons of our Lord the King of England of Winchelsea'. The device of the counter-seal shows the religious houses of the town of Winchelsea. The steps at the base of the central tower lead to a porch wherein is depicted the Annunciation of Our Lady. The three niches on the right of the tower show the murder of St Thomas of Canterbury and on the left are two niches illustrating St Giles with the hind he saved from the King's arrow.

103. (right) The royal arms of Winchelsea show three lions in gold on a red background and on the right-hand side are the prows of three silver ships on a blue background which represents the sea.

Local Landscapes and Buildings

104. Camber Castle, which earlier in its history was known as Winchelsea Castle. It is thought that the castle stands on the site of a more ancient building. Henry VIII built it at a cost of £23,000 to guard the approaches to Rye. Although it was originally on a spit of land it now stands, a lonely sentinel, in the middle of the marshes. It has one large tower, which also serves as the keep, surrounded by a number of smaller ones.

105. The Pipewell or Land Gate. This gate is of a later date than the two other town gates having been rebuilt in 1404 following its destruction by the French in 1380. The Pipewell Gate gave access to the ferry and later to the road which led from Winchelsea to Rye.

106. This artist's impression of Strand Gate was published in 1817. It was drawn by F. W. L. Stockdale and engraved by W. Wallis.

107. Strand Gate, c.1910.

108. New Gate from an early 19th-century engraving by Stockdale and Wallis. This gate is situated on the south side of the town, nearly a mile from the Strand Gate. It commands a spur of land which was formerly lapped on both sides by the high tide.

109. This photograph shows New Gate and a portion of the adjoining town wall in 1912. It remains little altered today.

110. (*left*) Court Hall, which may at one time have been occupied by the water bailiff. The building dates from various periods: the upper part and the roof are mainly 15th-century, and it is thought that the portion of the south front built of squared stones may have formed part of the house of Reginald Alard. Apparently the property was given to the church to supply the means to maintain lamps and candles but was confiscated at the Reformation. In 1587 Queen Elizabeth granted it to the town of Winchelsea in return for a small rental, and during the following century it was used as a town hall; the gaol may have been transferred there in the 18th century. About 1812 the property was apparently in the hands of Sir William Ashburnham and after passing through several ownerships was purchased by Mr. Freshfield, who presented it to the town in 1890. The mayoral election takes place here every Easter Monday with much of the ceremonial dating from the 13th century.

111. Detail from a picture on wooden panels in the Court House. This picture in distemper is thought to date from the 14th century. It depicts St Leonard blessing the fruits of the earth.

Cinque Ports
LOCAL MILITIA.

The Ancient Town of WINCHELSEA, in the County of Sussex, and the Liberties thereof.

NOTICE IS HEREBY GIVEN,

THAT the Cinque Ports Regiment of Local Militia, is ordered to assemble for Training and Exercise in the following order: Viz.

THE permanent Non-Commissioned Officers and Drummers and those Men enrolled in the said Militia within the said Town of WINCHELSEA, and the Liberties thereof WHO DID NOT assemble last Year, through Sickness or otherwise, and those who have since been enrolled, are particularly required and enjoined to assemble at *Deal in the County of Kent on Monday the twenty fifth day of this Instant May*

at the hour of NINE in the Morning; — then and there to present themselves to the Officer commanding the said Regiment, for the purpose of being Trained and Exercised, for the space or number of twenty one entire Days, exclusive of the Days of arriving at and departure from, and marching to and from the Place above mentioned and appointed or Muster, Training and Exercising.

AND all men enrolled in the said Militia within the said Town of WINCHELSEA, and the Liberties thereof, and who duly attended the Training and Exercise of the said Regiment last Year, are particularly required and enjoined to assemble at *Deal aforesaid on Monday the first day of June next*

at the hour of NINE in the Morning, then and there to present themselves to the Officer commanding the said Regiment, for the purpose of being Trained and Exercised for the space or number of fourteen entire Days, exclusive of the Days of arrival, departure, and marching as aforesaid. *Dated the sixth day of May 1812*

Carbell

TO

One of the Persons enrolled to serve for the Town of Winchelsea, and the Liberties thereof, in the Local Militia for the Cinque Ports, who is ordered and required, under the Pains and Penalties of the present existing Laws in that behalf duly to attend at the Time and Place, and for the purpose above-mentioned, according to the intent and meaning of the above Notice

---

Coleman, Printer, Rye.

112. A notice to the Cinque Ports local militia, dated 6 May 1812, calling the men of Winchelsea to assemble for exercise and training for a period of 14 days 'exclusive of the days of arrival, departure and marching'. It is interesting to note that this proclamation was printed in the neighbouring town of Rye.

113. A flock of sheep passing Court Hall early this century.

No.	Names	Date of Commitment / Cause	County or Parish	Trade	Age	Height	Hair	Eyes	Face		Remarks
13	Barton Wm	Decr 11, Breach during Revenue Measure	Rye Sussex	Fisherman	50	5/6	dark	Gray	long	slight	Discharged April 18
14	Clark Richd	do do do	Rye Sussex	Bargeman	48	5/4	Brown	Gray	long	slight	do 10th Feby 1832
15	Gibson Edwd	do do do	Rye Sussex	Fisherman	60	5/8	Gray	dark	long	stout	do 31 Decr
16	Pattenshaw Jno Sayle		Winchelsea Sussex	Labourer	26	5/6	Brown	dark	round	slight	do 11th Octr
		Year Ending Michs 29th Septr 1831									
17	Pigott Jno	Janry 26 Felton Vagrant	Winchelsea Sussex	Shoemaker	..	..	..	..	..	..	Removed to Lewes 7 Feby to take his trial
18	Rain Jno	April 8 Trespass 2 days	Udimore Sussex	Labourer	24	5/7	brown	black	round	high	dischargd 9 April
		Year Ending Michs 29th Septr 1832									
19	Barton Edwd	Novr 11 Vagrant 5 days	Rye Sussex	Labourer	27	5/7	Black	Black	round	stout	discharged 16 Nov
20	Rabey John	Nov 29 Breach during Revenue Measure on Call	Rye Sussex	Seaman	43	5/9	Brown	Gray	long	stout	do Aug 30th
21	Edwards Richd	Mard 25 Vagrant Month	Winchelsea Sussex	Labourer	25	5/8	Brown	Gray	round	slight	Removd to Battle gaol for Punishment
22	Hall Thos	Septr 21 misdem an 42 days	Winchelsea Sussex	Labourer	19	5/4	Black	Black	round	stout	discharged 31 Octr
23	Millard Henry	Septr 28 Breach Peace 14 day	Winchelsea Sussex	Labourer	20	5/8	Light	dark	round	stout	do 11th Octr
		Year Ending Michs 29th Septr 1833									
24	Amon Wm	April 4 Vagrant 3 days	Winchelsea Sussex		50	5/3	dark	dark	long	stout	do 7th April
25	Vagrants two	May 20 do	Boys								do 27 May
26	do two	June 24 do									do 25 June
		Year Ending Michs 29th Septr 1834									

114. This page from the Winchelsea gaol book records the names of those individuals who were unfortunate enough to be imprisoned for their crimes. Where these were of a more serious nature a prisoner was either 'Removed to Battle gaol for Punishment' or sent to Lewes to stand trial. Miscreants rarely occupied this prison for longer than six months. It is interesting to note that certain of the wrongdoers' crimes was described as 'Breach of Revenue'; this may refer to smuggling which was rife in the area at this time.

115. The High Street, looking towards Strand Gate and the marshes beyond, c.1900.

116. (*right*) The Old Workhouse at the bottom of Strand Hill, c.1900. The first work of Drake Hollinbury, who became rector of Winchelsea in 1792, was to reform the workhouse. Later in its history this building became a guest house.

117. (*below*) The large building on the right of this early 20th-century picture is the armoury, undoubtedly the oldest private building in Winchelsea. Although the house has been much restored this century, the Gothic archway, walls and floors are reputed to be contemporaneous with the building of the town. The large square building abutting it is the town well. A notice dated 1832 states that 'the well closed 7 p.m. and opened 6 a.m. Closed ALL day on the Sabbath' —presumably the inhabitants were expected to use the other wells on this day!

118. (*right*) The town well was of great importance as it was the only public well actually within the town walls. The little building housing the well and tackle is an interesting survival from an earlier age. It still exhibits its 19th-century notice boards whose instructions remained valid until the introduction of piped water allowed the well to fall into disuse.

119. This photograph taken at the turn of the century shows F. Crisford & Son, Family Butchers of Mill Road.

120. The old bakery, now Manna Plat. During the last century many people had ovens too small to cook their weekly joint so they took them to the local baker who cooked them in his oven for a small charge. Earlier there had been a large bakery oven situated near the armoury but this was demolished some years ago.

121. The old *Bridge Inn* at the foot of Strand Hill c.1890. It is interesting to speculate on the early ways of advertising before the onset of the media.

122. The *New Inn* at the turn of the century when there were shops in German Street. At one time there were three inns in the town: The *Salutation* was one of the original taverns and is said to have been built on the foundations of an inn dating from 1288.

123. (*left*) An ancient house known as 'Five Chimneys', c.1904. The chimney shown in this photograph was removed before 1941 when the house was bombed during World War II. It was rebuilt in 1947.

124. (*below*) This painting of the mill is by Arthur Foord Hughes (born 1856), who was trained in the Pre-Raphaelite school and specialised in painting windmills throughout Sussex. Fairlight may be seen in the distance.

125. (*opposite page, above*) The coastguard station at Winchelsea beach c.1922.

126. (*opposite page, below*) The Grey Friars, or Franciscans, were established in Old Winchelsea soon after the order arrived in England in 1224. When the town was destroyed by the sea the Grey Friars accompanied the townsfolk to their new quarters on Iham Hill. The benefactors of the Winchelsea house included the town's most eminent merchants and landowners. Following the dissolution of the monasteries during the reign of Henry VIII ornaments and furniture were removed from the house and it passed into the custody of Captain Philip Chowte, at that time captain of Camber Castle. The cells and chapel, however, were not wholly destroyed. This picture, drawn in 1785, shows the ruins of part of the chapel.

Religion

127. Grey Friars Chapel and adjoining house. Built in 1819, the house was enlarged and restored later in the century and in 1910 a handsome loggia was erected. At one time it was the home of Mr. G. M. Freeman 'to whom Winchelsea and all those who would preserve the beauty and interest of England owe a great debt of gratitude', as W. MacLean Homan stated in 1936 in his *History and Antiquities of Winchelsea*. The building now belongs to East Sussex County Council and is used as a home for the elderly.

128. Gardeners at work in the grounds of Grey Friars, c.1900.

Winchelsea Church

129.   The church of St Thomas the Martyr of Canterbury from a lithograph by S. Hooper published in 1785. Until the end of the 18th century this ruined tower stood in the south-west side of the churchyard. The origin and use of this tower are unknown. It may have been a campanile or bell-tower but a more likely explanation is that it was raised for the defence of the town of Iham in Saxon times, before the church itself was built.

130. St Thomas a Becket's church from a painting which hangs in Winchelsea museum.

131. (*above*) Winchelsea church from a drawing by L. Nixon published as an engraving by Edward Harding of 98 Pall Mall, London, in 1801.

132. (*left*) The interior of Winchelsea church c.1880.

133. It is believed that ten of these 'bumping stones' survive. Originally they defined the ecclesiastical parish of St Leonard, adjoining modern Winchelsea. The name 'bumping stone' is said to derive from the story that choir boys were 'bumped' on these stones during the ceremony of beating the bounds, to impress on them the limits of their parish. The lettering 'CH' upon all the stones probably represents 'Corporation of Hastings', since that town was the holder of the parliamentary franchise of the parish of St Leonard.

134. This painting by an unknown artist shows the tree under which John Wesley preached his last sermon in the open air on 7 October 1790. He made the following entry in his journal: 'I went over to that poor skeleton of ancient Winchelsea. It is beautifully situated on the top of a steep hill, and was regularly built in broad streets, crossing each other, and encompassing a very large square, in the midst of which was a large church, now in ruins. I stood under a large tree on the side of it, and called to most of the inhabitants of the town: "The kingdom of heaven is at hand, repent, and believe the gospel". It seemed as if all that heard were, at the present, almost persuaded to be Christians'. The ash tree was uprooted in 1927, but another has replaced it.

135. (*left*) This goblet was turned from part of the ash tree under which John Wesley preached his last sermon in the open air.

136. (*right*) Asenath Jones was 84 years of age when this photograph was taken in 1867. When John Wesley preached at Winchelsea in 1790 he was the guest of Mr. Jones, Asenath's father. The chair is the one in which Wesley sat with Asenath on his knee, and is always regarded as the Preacher's Chair.

Education

137. This photograph shows the interior of Winchelsea school in 1937 (note the doors have been folded back in order to incorporate the two classrooms into one for the purpose of this picture). The then headmistress, Miss Lilah Smith, who served the school for so many years, is seated at her desk. In 1815 provision was made for the formal education of poor children between the ages of six and 14 in a thatched building on the north side of Winchelsea, giving its name to the present 'School Hill'. The State assumed responsibility for general education in 1870 and the Church in Winchelsea took advantage of this financial help in 1873 to build a new and larger school at the east side of St Thomas's church. The Rector, Edward Whitehead, held the glebe property on which the school was to be built and sold it to himself and the churchwardens for £46 19s. By 1964 the building had become unsafe and the site for a new one was secured. Pupils were transferred from the old school in 1966 and the formal opening by Lady Winifred Paget took place on the eve of St Thomas's Day, 5 July 1968.

138. (*above*) Lace making school, c.1900. The school was started by Mrs. Skinner of Periteau House about 1898. Lace making was a traditional cottage industry but was hit later by the introduction of machinery. The teacher in this picture is Mrs. Cook and the girls are, from left to right: (*seated*) Annie Venness, Venetia Sachse, Daisy Wheeler, Annie Griffin; (*standing*) ? Carter and Annie Homard.

139. (*left*) Lace was being made in Winchelsea during the 18th and early 19th centuries, chiefly by small children apprenticed there by the Overseers of the Poor in neighbouring parishes.

Occasions and Personalities

140.   Thomas Denman (1779 - 1854). In 1820 he became
Queen Caroline's solicitor-general and actively assisted in her
successful defence against the attempt to divorce her. He was
elevated to the peerage in 1834.

141. Queen Caroline was estranged from her husband, the Prince Regent, for many years. On his accession to the throne efforts were made to dissolve the marriage.

142. Henry Peter Brougham (1778 - 1868). In 1816 Brougham became one of the two representatives of Winchelsea in the House of Commons until elevated to the peerage. In 1820, with the support of Thomas Denman, he successfully defended the Queen against the attempt to dissolve her marriage to the new king, George IV.

143.   A 19th-century inhabitant of Winchelsea, Mrs. (Granny) Smith. It is interesting to speculate whether the lace around her elaborate bonnet was made in Winchelsea.

144. (*right*) Dame Ellen Terry
(1847 - 1928), who for a number of
years lived in Tower Cottage. She
first appeared on the stage in 1856
as Mamillius in Shakespeare's *The
Winter's Tale*. She was married three
times and had two children. Her
friendship with Henry Irving commenced in 1878 and remained
unbroken until 1902. He was a
frequent visitor to Tower Cottage,
which she retained until 1914. In
1899 Ellen Terry bought Smallhythe
Place near Tenterden and divided her
time between the two houses. She was
known as 'the painters' actress', for
Watts, Burne-Jones and Sargent
immortalised her. Unfortunately, she
never found time to sit for Millais who
at one time also lived in Winchelsea.
For a while Ellen Terry advised and
attended the town's own amateur
theatricals, and she was also known
for her good works: at one point during the early part of this century she
was reputed to have shod every child
in Winchelsea.

145. (*below*) Tower Cottage.

146. A cycling club assembled by Pipewell Gate, c.1890. Cycling was extremely popular with members of both sexes and they often travelled long distances on club outings.

147. This photograph of c.1916 shows a battalion of the King's Own Liverpool Light Infantry marching at Winchelsea where they were stationed for a time during the first World War.

148. (*right*) Mr. Turner, who became mayor in 1983 was only the second one this century to have been born and bred in Winchelsea. The names of former mayors are recorded on a series of oak boards now housed in the museum. This list dates from 1295, when mayors first replaced the king's bailiffs, but until 1430 it is only partially complete. Following an early 19th-century inquiry into alleged maladministration Winchelsea not only lost the right to return two members to Parliament but was stripped of her magisterial and other functions. The Corporation was however allowed to remain in existence in order to administer a sum of less than twenty pounds per annum derived from town rents and royal dues. A mayor and other corporate officials continue to be elected for this purpose at a Hundred Court held at the ancient Court Hall on Easter Monday.

149. (*below*) Princess Elizabeth with her parents, then the Duke and Duchess of York, in the doorway of St Thomas a Becket's church during their visit to the town in 1935. Princess Margaret, who would have been five years old at this time, was obviously felt to be too young to undertake public duties.

150. Queen Elizabeth II with the mayor, Mr. David Homan, during her visit to Winchelsea in 1966.

CHRONOLOGICAL TABLE OF MAIN EVENTS
IN THE HISTORY OF RYE

(Source for 1002-1935 L. A. Vidler, A New History of Rye, 2nd ed., 1971)

c. 1002	King Ethelred II promised and King Canute granted by charter lands, including the town of Rye, to the Abbey of Fecamp in Normandy.
c. 1030	King Canute granted advowson of church of St Mary, Rye to Abbot of Fecamp.
1086	Domesday Survey shows Rye entered under the possessions of the Church of Fecamp.
c. 1189	Simon the Priest appointed by Abbot of Fecamp to be Warden of St Bartholomew's Hospital, Rye.
1213	Two ships furnished by Rye to Cinque Ports Navy took part in the naval victory over the French in the harbour of Damme.
1216	Aubrey de Den and Geoffrey de Craucombe resumed Rye and Winchelsea and in 1249 appointed the Barons of Rye.
1220	The French captured merchandise and wine from Rye.
1226	First document executed to exchange English possessions with French.
1223	Men from Rye and Winchelsea man five ships of the Cinque Port Fleet.
1243	Permanent building erected for King's galleys. These were previously berthed at Winchelsea.
1247	Charter of Resumption (exchange) of Rye and Winchelsea to King of England.
1249	Building of Ypres Tower commences.
1250	Sea walls completed. Rye Charters commence.
1263	Friars of the Sack came to town.
1270	The Barons of Rye granted £50 to Prince Edward for Crusade.
c. 1270	First recorded water mills for grinding corn. Court of Justice, presided over by the Bailiff. Market Place. Dues on the shares of the fishing fleet charged at fixed rate.
1275	Rye passed into the hands of the Dowager Queen.
1279	Foundation of the Chantry of St Nicholas.
1287	River Rother changed course from outlet at Romney Haven to Rye.
1289	King Edward I regained Rye from his mother. Robert Paulin appointed Bailiff of Rye and the town incorporated.
1290	Yearly fair held on the feast of the Nativity of St Mary.
1307	Elias Muriel, Baron of Rye received special permission to export corn and other victuals and to import wine from Gascony.
1329	Murage Grants resulted in building the town walls, Landgate, Strand gate, Baddings gate and Postern gate.
1339	Rye sacked by French.
1348-1350	First Rectory House and first Town Hall recorded.
1349	Black Death, Rye Battery appeared to be abandoned.
1350	Battle of Rye Bay, Edward III and Black Prince against the Spaniards.
1360	Rye again invaded by French.
1364	Founding of first house of the Friars Heremites of St Austin in Rye.
1360-69	Black Death — no evidence of incidents in the town during the later years of the scourge.
1366	William Taillour and Richard Baddyng first recorded members of parliament.
1377	Rye captured by French, who planned to ravage surrounding countryside, defied by Abbot of Battle. Rye church left a roofless ruin.
1378	Men of Rye and Winchelsea sacked French towns in Normandy and recovered much of booty taken from them, including Rye church bells.
1379	Chapel and Manse of St Austin being undermined by sea, friars moved to a new site called 'La Haltone'.

1394	A tripartite agreement between Hastings, Rye and Winchelsea as to the number of ships they should supply to Cinque Port Fleet. These were Hastings five, Rye five and Winchelsea 10.
1403	Market days changed from Wednesday and Friday to Wednesday and Saturday.
pre-1415	Custumal of Rye.
1416	Three hundred ships of the Cinque Port Fleet assembled at Sandwich and Rye before going to the relief of Harfleur.
1425	The ripiers (carriers and retailers of fish) liable to dues.
1430	All animals illegally entering churchyard made their owners liable to a fine of 3s. 4d. the money being put towards the fabric of the church. The Tower (now called Ypres) sold to John de Iprys as a residence.
1447	Manor of Lewisham (later Leasam) let. This was one of the first documents drawn up and written in English.
1449	Tenterden incorporated with Rye.
1488	King Henry VII visits Rye.
1489	Ships built at Rye for the King.
1497	'Wagge' bell purchased from Wm. Culendon, Bellfounder of London.
1502	New mace made.
1513	Churchwardens' Accounts commence.
1518	The town purchased Ypres Tower for £26, described as 'Baddings Towre alia Ipres Tower'.
1521	Conduit made from Playden Hill along Rope Walk and up Conduit Hill into the town.
1528	The names of the 37 Freemen who attended the meeting at the Cross in the Churchyard are recorded for the first time.
1538	Austin Friary suppressed; remained in King's hands until 1545, when all the buildings and property were sold to Thomas Goodwyn.
1541	Camber Castle armed with necessary artillery and a captain appointed.
1548	The Chantry of St Nicholas suppressed.
1551	Alexander Wellys 'donated land without the Landgate' for the 'decaying, sick and feeble'.
1552	The courthouse (which may at this time have been housed in the Ypres Tower) was repaired.
1554	Father John Browne, the last Roman Catholic to officiate in the parish church of Rye took office. He died in 1557.
1556	The principal market at this time was at the Strand, where storehouses and a crane were erected.
1557-1559	Rye bought guns and overhauled her ordnance.
1562-3	Protestant refugees arrive in the town.
1563	Plague strikes Rye (562 persons buried).
1572	Main influx of refugees after the massacre of St Bartholomew. At this time there were 1,534 people of French extraction living in the town. Queen Elizabeth I visits Rye and Winchelsea.
1576	Mayor and jurats trod out the bounds of the Liberties of the town and marked them with stones.
1579	John Fletcher the dramatist born in Rye.
1580	Further outbreaks of plague.
1586	Rye outfits one ship for Queen, but it took no part in the defeat of the Armada.
1588	'Watch' appointed in Rye.
1603	Robert Wood the first mayor to be elected in the Guildhall and not at the Old Cross in the Churchyard, as previously.
1632	Thomas Brown and his descendants purchased land from the Indians in 1660 and founded two villages, Rye and Hastings in New York State.
1638	Thomas Peacocke, jurat, died and in his will left provision for the founding of a Free School for the boys of Rye.
1623	Birth of Samuel Jeake. First historian of Rye, he died in 1690.
1652-1668	Rye tokens minted.
1657	Foot soldiers quartered in Rye, men of Col. Rb. Gibbons Regiment.
1660	Rye takes precedence over Winchelsea by virtue of the Brotherhood. 1660 Census.

1661	Thomas Watson appointed first master of the Free Grammar School.
1682–1685	More French Protestants arrive in the town.
1690	Repairs to town and postern gates carried out. Turnpike erected to prevent passage of horses, in order to control traffic in the town.
1701	Letters Patent granted for permission to collect towards repairs to church. Work complete 1703.
1717	First association of the name 'Lamb' with the town, being the marriage of Martha Grebell to James Lamb. Lime kiln built in town, voted a public nuisance and subsequently demolished.
1721	Free School founded on non-sectarian lines, by the will of James Saunders of Winchelsea. Licences granted to many inns in Rye. However, the oldest Rye inn records relate to the two inns which were conveniently close to the Court Hall in the Butchery, the *George* (on its previous site) and the *Red Lyon* [*sic*]. Records for both date from the mid-16th century.
1725	Storm in Rye Bay. George I took refuge in the town and presented a godson (born during his enforced visit) with a silver bowl inscribed 'The Gift of His Majesty King George to his Godson, George Lambe Anno dom. 1725'.
1731	Further water pipes laid from Saltcote Cliff to the Postern conduit — later erection of Water Tower in Churchyard.
1735	Gungarden Gate dismantled, Portcullis removed from Landgate.
1742	Old Court Hall and Market Place (two separate buildings) demolished. New Town Hall built. Allen Grebell (a past mayor of Rye) murdered in mistake for his brother-in-law James Lamb.
1700–1754	Bridges over Tillingham and Brede rivers built.
1757	William Duke of Cumberland, 3rd son of King, inspected the defences of the town. Gunner again appointed to take care of the cannons. Brass cannon moved to the Green (at the end of Watchbell Street).
1758	Memorandum of Agreement signed — all applicants supported each other as candidates for the mayoralty. When discovered in 1825 this led to the impetus of the Reform movement in Rye.
1759	Edward Dengate built mill, later known as 'Fisher Clark's Mill' on land leased from Corporation. This mill burnt down *c.* 1879.
1763 onwards	Town walls demolished and Strand Gate likewise.
1769	John Smeaton commences work on new harbour. In 1787 Rother and Tillingham turned into new harbour. By 1788 all work abandoned.
1758–1790	John Wesley visits Rye.
1773	Wesley preached in a building in Mermaid Street, which was formerly erected by Mrs. Jeake for the Presbyterians.
1779	Cinque Port Volunteers Company raised for Rye, disbanded 1773.
1789	Wesleyan Chapel opened.
1791	New Wharf on Strand.
1794	Cinque Port Volunteers reformed, again disbanded in 1808.
1801	H.R.H. Duke of York reviewed troops stationed on Strand and at Rye Hill.
c. 1802	Rye theatre in Cinque Port Street opened with *Richard III.*
1807	Rye vessel the *Chiswell* lying off Dungeness waiting for high tide in order to enter Rye Harbour lost with all hands.
1819	Town gaol in Ypres Tower repaired.
1824	All prisoners committed for periods of over one month sent to Battle gaol.
1825	Two Mayors of Rye, the Rev. Wm. Dobson and Mr. John Meryon, the usurper, who held his position for six weeks.
1826	Rye Independent Association constituted in area.
1830	Colonel de Lacey Evans stands for reformers against Corporation candidate Philip Pusey.
1832	Rye lost one M.P. with the passing of the Reform Bill. Edward Jeremiah Curteis elected M.P. by a majority of 34.
1833	Embankment Act. Corporation built the sea wall from Fishmarket to Pollards Wharf enclosed Town and North Salts, which later became recreation grounds.
1835	An Act to Provide for the Regulation of Municipal Corporations in England and Wales brought to an end the method by which the town had been governed since 1289.

1835 *cont.*	Councillor David Manser first Mayor to be elected under this Act.
1845	Proposed railway line from Ashford through Rye to Hastings.
1850	Opening of the railway and the iron swing bridge over the Rother. The Hon. T. Farncombe, Lord Mayor of London performed the ceremony. Building of new almshouses in Military Road.
1852	Complaints made against the quality of the gas lighting, which had been installed in the town in 1846, 25 lamp standards at that time being considered sufficient. Rye electors bribed; matter became an inquiry before the House of Commons; Jeremiah Smith, agent for the Liberal candidate, was subsequently reprieved.
1855	Gas laid to town hall.
1856	Two Free Schools in Rye united.
1859	Cinque Ports Volunteer Rifle corps formed. Later became known as the 3rd Cinque Ports Rifle Volunteers.
1862	Three local newspapers, the *Rye Chronicle*, the *Rye Free Press* and the *Rye Telegram*, all printed locally. Clock placed in the Landgate in memory of Prince Consort.
1866	Volunteer Fire Brigade formed. National School built in Mermaid Street. Frederick Mitchell started a pottery in Ferry Road, thus carrying out work which had commenced as early as the 13th century in and around Rye. Steam engine installed in pump-house in Cinque Port street, to pump water to the cistern in the churchyard, work previously done by horsepower.
1869	Soup kitchen built against the Ypres Tower; it was subsequently demolished.
1870	Death of William Holloway, the historian of Rye.
1882	Extremely high tide flooded all the low lying areas of the town.
1887	Scheme mooted for building a bridge and road connecting Rye with East Guldeford. Monkbretton Bridge opened in 1893.
1888	Rye Regatta revived — flourished for a number of years.
c. 1894	Golf course opened at Camber.
1895	Rye and Camber Tramway constructed connecting the Club with the Monkbretton Bridge.
1900	Roman Catholic Church, St Walburga, built, subsequently demolished 1927.
1905	Austin Friary acquired by a syndicate and converted into a Church House.
1907	New Grammar School built.
1912	Drill Hall and Armoury opened.
1915	Hospital for war wounded opened in upper room of the Austin Friary. Air raid on Rye Harbour.
1921	Rye and District Memorial Hospital opened.
1922	County Court removed to Hastings.
c. 1925	Battery House and Gungarden purchased from the War Office by the Corporation for a sum of £1,550. Later the former housed Rye Museum.
1928	Rye Harbour Lifeboat disaster. All hands lost.
1929	R.C. Church of St Anthony of Padua opened. Next year Convent School opened.
1935	Queen Mary visits town.
1939	Closure of Rye and Camber Tramway to civilian traffic.
1940–45	Town sustained bomb damage to various well-known buildings, including the Wesleyan chapel, roof of Ypres Tower, *Mermaid* Inn and Strand House.
1966	Visit of Queen Elizabeth II and Duke of Edinburgh.
1974	Rye 'lost' borough status after 800 years when Bexhill-on-Sea, Rye and Battle amalgamated under the Local Government Act becoming Rother D.C. The two first-named continued to appoint their own mayors.
1980	Queen Elizabeth the Queen Mother in her capacity as Lord Warden of the Cinque Ports, visits the town.
1982	Second visit of Queen Elizabeth the Queen Mother.

Population Tables and Acreage of Rye and Winchelsea

	Rye acreage 2,462 acres	*Winchelsea 965 acres*
	Population	Population
1801	2,187	627
1811	2,581	652
1821	3,599	817
1831	3,715	772
1841	4,031	687
1851	4,592	778
1861	4,288	719
1871	4,366	679
1881	4,667	613
1891	4,368	686
1901	4,337	670
*1911	4,229	1,449
1921	3,920	1,474
1931	4,058	1,583
1941	—	—
1951	4,509	1,797
1961	4,438	1,974
1971	4,449	2,039
1981	4,281	2,331

Sources: *V.C.H.* 2, p. 96 (for 1801–1901) and E.S.C.C. County Hall, Lewes (for 1911–1981)

* From this date Winchelsea was included with Winchelsea Beach and Rye Harbour in Icklesham Parish; this accounts for the higher population statistics shown here.